A TASTE of the PAST

INTERNATIONAL·HORSE·SHOW
OLYMPIA·LONDON·JUNE 17-29,1912

CLARIDGE'S
HOTEL

A TASTE
of the
PAST

JOHN LANE

David & Charles

A DAVID & CHARLES BOOK
David & Charles is a subsidiary of F+W (UK) Ltd.,
an F+W Publications Inc. company

First published in the UK in 2004

Copyright © John Lane 2004

Distributed in North America
by F+W Publications, Inc.
4700 East Galbraith Road
Cincinnati, OH 45236
1-800-289-0963

John Lane has asserted his right to be identified as author
of this work in accordance with the Copyright, Designs and
Patents Act, 1988.

A catalogue record for this book is available from the
British Library.

ISBN 0 7153 1842 X

Printed in China by SNP Leefung
for David & Charles
Brunel House   Newton Abbot   Devon

Commissioning Editor Jane Trollope
Senior Editor Freya Dangerfield
Designer Lisa Forrester
Production Controller Jennifer Campbell

Visit our website at www.davidandcharles.co.uk

David & Charles books are available from all good
bookshops; alternatively you can contact our Orderline
on (0)1626 334555 or write to us at FREEPOST EX2 110,
David & Charles Direct, Newton Abbot, TQ12 4ZZ (no
stamp required UK mainland).

Contents

Introduction

This lavishly illustrated book is the fruit of a lifetime's collection of menu cards. John Lane is the son of a chef, and as a young man was privileged to attend professional chefs' banquets with his father. This led to a life-long interest in banquets and the menu cards which are the *mementos* of such occasions. The field they cover is enormous. His main interest is in the menus for *royal banquets*, and the book illustrates a selection of royal wedding breakfasts, as well as Queen Victoria's Golden and Diamond Jubilees and various banquets given for visiting heads of state. But there are also menus shown from grand hotels, famous restaurants and ocean liners. These *beautifully illustrated* cards are *historic documents*, commemorating such events as the Boat Race of 1897, a dinner given in 1864 to honour the Italian General Garibaldi, and another in 1909 to honour US President Ulysses Grant. We see the inception of the Entente Cordiale, the diplomatic attempts to avert World War I, and the Victory Dinner given in 1946 for holders of the Victoria Cross.

There are also more lighthearted occasions: Christmas Day 1923 at the Hotel Cecil in London, *a taste of luxury* from the Royal Hawaiian Hotel in Honolulu, 1929, and a banquet given by the Aéro-Club of France at the Palais d'Orsay Hotel in Paris in 1924, attended by Louis Blériot, the first man to fly across the Channel.

A HISTORY OF MENUS

Menu is a French word meaning bill of fare. It is not known whether it originated in France or England, but in England it first appears as a concept in the reign of Henry VIII, at a banquet given by the Duke of Brunswick in 1541. It was noticed that the Duke from time to time consulted a piece of paper which lay on the table. When asked what it was, he explained that it was a list of the dishes to be served. He consulted it, just as we do now, in order to conserve his appetite for those dishes he liked best. This idea was greatly admired, and soon became generally adopted.

Dinners at this time consisted of two courses, each of 40 or so dishes which were laid on the table at the same time. The first was the *entrée*, so called because the dishes were set on the table before the diners entered the room. The second course was the *relevé*, or remove, which relieved, or followed, the first course, after it had been removed. Gradually, dinners were divided into more courses, though they retained the names entrée and remove, or *relevé*. The name *entremets* appeared, covering dishes which were not soup, entrée or remove, such as vegetable dishes, jellies, puddings, pastries, salads, lobsters and prawns.

A State Banquet at Windsor Castle given by Queen Elizabeth II in honour of President Reagan, 1982.

At first there was one large menu at the end of the table, sometimes beautifully illustrated. This was later reduced in size and more copies were made available. As the menu evolved it became more of a presentation to the guest. They were sometimes painted on silk or parchment, making a souvenir for the diner. The individual menu appeared in the early 19th century. It was adopted by celebrated restaurants, particularly in Paris, where they commissioned artists to illustrate these menus by hand. Even great artists such as Renoir would consent to do this.

Although most menus are printed or handwritten on stiff card, many other materials have been used over the years, including silk, papier mâché and paper lace. A charming example of a paper lace menu is the one produced for the banquet in honour of General Garibaldi, held at the Fishmongers Hall in London 1864 (left, and page 56). The beautifully decorated menu for Queen Victoria's Diamond Jubilee is handwritten (above left and page 40), as is the menu for King Edward's shooting party at Sandringham in 1904 (page 44).

Mrs Beeton says in her celebrated book *Household Management* (1861) that a formal dinner should have eight courses: hors-d'oeuvre, soup (usually a clear and a thick soup), fish, entrée (hot dishes served before cold ones), remove (such as

COLD COLLATION DISHES.

1—Pigeon Pie. 2—Raised Game Pie. 3—Cutlets and Peas. 4—Prawns en Bouquet. 5—Crème Chicken. 6—Plovers' Eggs. 7—Lamb Cutlets. 8—Larks Farcie. 9—Piped Ham. 10—Boned Capon.

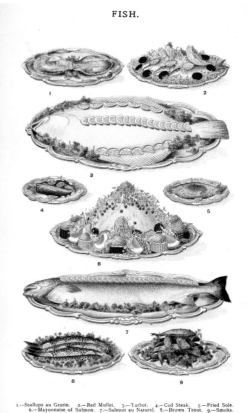

FISH.

1.—Scallops au Gratin. 2.—Red Mullet. 3.—Turbot. 4.—Cod Steak. 5.—Fried Sole. 6.—Mayonnaise of Salmon. 7.—Salmon au Naturel. 8.—Brown Trout. 9.—Smelts.

Far left: Examples of cold dishes from Mrs Beeton's Household Management *(1861).*

Left: Fish dishes from the same book.

Below: Example of a table setting from Mrs Beeton.

joints, ducks, geese, chickens etc), roasts (usually poultry or game, such as pheasant, partridge etc) again the hot served before the cold, entremets (which covers vegetable dishes, puddings, sweets and savouries) and dessert, which includes fresh and dried fruit, nuts, bonbons and petit fours, and fancy biscuits.

Not all the Victorian and Edwardian menus illustrated here have eight courses, but they almost always have the soup, fish, entrée, remove and entremets, together with the buffet or cold table. The first menu in this book, dated 1874, is for a dinner at Windsor Castle celebrating the marriage of Queen Victoria's son Alfred to the Grand Duchess Marie of Russia (page 18). It has five courses, plus a buffet of roast meats, something that features in many of the Victorian menus.

The Victorians, of course, were noted for their hearty appetites and this continued into the Edwardian age. The Prince of Wales, later King Edward VII, was famous for his gargantuan appetite. He consumed five meals a day and was known affectionately as Tum Tum. The dinner given in his honour in 1903 at the Élysée Palace in Paris (page 42) had 18 dishes, including such rich fare as tartlets with crayfish in a cream sauce, salmon trout, baron of lamb, grouse sautéed in sherry, ducklings, foie gras with brandy and truffles and asparagus in a cream sauce. It was (and still is) customary at such elaborate dinners to serve a liqueur sorbet halfway through, to aid digestion. This is known as a *trou* (hole), the theory being that it makes room for the rest of the meal!

This formula of at least five courses lasted though the 1920s and 1930s right up to the outbreak of World War II. The dinner menus of the great liners of the period, such as the one for the *Queen Mary*'s maiden voyage (page 87) are noticeably lavish, as are those of the grand hotels, such as the Palace Hotel in San Francisco (page 144) or Claridge's in London (page 150).

Menus since then have been shorter and simpler, even for state occasions or royal wedding breakfasts. The state banquet given at Buckingham Palace for President Chirac has four courses (page 72), while the wedding breakfasts of both Prince Charles and Princess Diana and the Duke and Duchess of York have only three courses apiece (pages 26–31).

Above: Menu for the banquet held at Windsor Castle 1874 to celebrate the marriage of Queen Victoria's son Prince Alfred to the Grand Duchess Marie of Russia.

The short, simple menu for the wedding breakfast of the Duke and Duchess of York in 1986.

Menu

Oeufs Drumkilbo

Carré d'Agneau Paloise
Couronne d'Epinards aux Champignons
Fèves au Beurre
Pommes Nouvelles

Salade

Fraises St. George
Crème Caillée

Les Vins

Piesporter Goldtröpfchen Auslese 1976
Château Langoa Barton 1976
Bollinger 1966
Graham 1966

READING MENUS

By the early 19th century, when individual menus first appeared, Paris was recognized as a gastronomic centre and so the convention began of printing menus in French. This French domination of cuisine continued through the 19th century and most of the 20th century, largely due to the influence of two notable chefs. It was Antoine Carême, born in Paris in 1784, who was really the founder of grand cuisine, the classic French cookery. Later in the 19th century came the famous chef Escoffier, who in association with César Ritz opened the Savoy Hotel in London in 1890. Both chefs wrote cookery books which became bibles of the culinary art. One of the menu cards shown is for a dinner given in London in honour of Escoffier in 1909 (right and page 96).

The convention of menu French has lasted up to the present day, though menus now often contain a mixture of French and English, or will be solely in English if the dishes are native English or American. Menu French is quite a challenge, even to French speakers, and so we have provided in this book a translation of each menu to help the reader.

Dishes or foods are sometimes named after certain regions or towns where they are noted for their excellence, such as Rouen duck, Marenne or Whitstable oysters, and Pauillac lamb. They may also be named after famous chefs or noted gourmets. Several dishes in these menus are named after Dugléré, a pupil of Carême who became Chef de Cuisine to the Rothschild family. Chicken Demidoff, an elaborate chicken dish, is named after a Russian, Prince Demidoff, who was a famous gourmet at the time of the French Second Empire. Chefs down the years have also delighted in naming dishes after well-known clients, famous examples being two dishes created by Escoffier: Pêche Melba (after Nellie Melba, the opera singer) and Tournedos Rossini (after the composer). But sometimes the famous client has disappeared from view, there is no record of the recipe, and we now have no idea what the dish is, except that it is a soup or a salad etc: Glace Viviane, an ice or ice cream, in the banquet given for King Edward VII in 1903 (page 42), is a case in point.

Chefs also delight in being whimsical or ultra-patriotic, giving dishes fancy names in honour of the occasion. Some examples are wild strawberries Margaret Rose in the 1937 Coronation menu in honour of Princess Margaret (page 52), the soup Double Victory and the Cinderella potatoes on the New Year menu at Quaglino's in 1939 (page 104), and the sole Santa Claus on the Christmas Day menu at the Hotel Cecil in 1923 (page 134).

SALADS.

1.—Cucumber. 2.—Beetroot and Potato. 3.—Macédoine. 4.—Tomato. 5.—Russian.
6.—Italian. 7.—Prawn. 8.—Egg. 9.—Lobster. 10.—Salad Dumas.

Left: Illustration of salads from Mrs Beeton's Household Management.

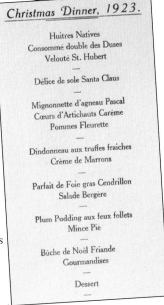

Above top: Menu for the dinner given in Paris in 1903 for King Edward VII (page 42); middle: New Year's Eve menu at Quaglino's, London 1939 (page 104); bottom: Christmas Dinner menu for 1923 at the Hotel Cecil, London (page 134).

12

THE AUTHOR'S COLLECTION

My interest in menus began over 30 years ago, when I attended formal dinners with my father, who at that time was principal lecturer at Westminster Catering College, the first hotel school, founded in 1910. Prior to that he had been a sous-chef at the Savoy Hotel, London.

A contemporary at the Savoy was Ronald Aubery, who in 1937 entered the royal household at Buckingham Palace and then in 1952 was appointed head chef to Queen Elizabeth II, the first Englishman to hold the appointment since records began in the 1820s. It was customary to employ additional experienced chefs to help at state banquets and royal wedding breakfasts, and so my father was asked to assist Ronald Aubery on these occasions. My father was also a member of the *Conseil Culinaire*, the French Council of Chefs, which held a banquet each year at a London hotel, attended by top chefs from Europe and the US. As a young man I was privileged to attend these banquets, magnificent occasions where there was obviously much rivalry, each hotel vying to be the best.

This unique experience of fine dining had a lasting effect, and later I turned to collecting menu cards, perhaps to recapture the magic of these occasions. It has proved to be a fascinating and rewarding hobby.

Above: John Lane's father with a student at Westminster Catering College.

'When I was a boy I was lucky enough on one occasion to go with my brother and my father to visit Ronald Aubery at Buckingham Palace, and he showed us around the banqueting rooms and the kitchens …The highlight of my visit to Buckingham Palace was to be beyond my wildest dreams. Mr Aubery asked me and my brother if we would like to see the gold plate and the gold ornaments that were used at the state banquets for visiting kings, queens and heads of state. After getting the key from a member of the royal household he led the way to a locked room. It was just like Aladdin's cave – tables were covered with gold ornaments, plates, knives, forks, vases, wine decanters and centrepieces.'

Above left: John Lane (third from right) and his father (fifth from right) at a dinner of the Association Culinaire Française at the Dorchester, London, 1967. John's wife is seated between them.

Gold dinner service.

COLLECTING MENU CARDS

Collecting menu cards can be a very interesting and rewarding hobby. They can be obtained from a number of different sources, such as dealers in ephemera, specialist book dealers (cookery books), Internet auction sites, and general auctions.

One of the best ways of starting a collection is to be given the menus. Ask your friends to save a menu card from their next holiday. If they are going on a cruise, the ocean liner companies are quite happy to let people have souvenir menus, as it is good advertising. A collection can be built up very cheaply this way. Make your interest known to as many people as possible and your collection will soon grow. Quite often people have menus tucked away in a drawer that they would be quite happy to part with. Book dealers sometimes acquire miscellaneous ephemera when they buy books, and are often quite happy to part with them cheaply. Antique dealers too can acquire menus with other stock, and car boot sales sometimes produce the odd piece of ephemera, including menus.

The interest in menus as historical documents has increased over the years. When I started my collection over 30 years ago there were not many collectors in this field, which made them much more difficult to find, but it had the advantage that they could be bought more cheaply. Now the interest is world-wide, as is the interest in all ephemera, and it is growing daily with the realization that these documents represent social history and should be preserved for future generations, whether it is a menu, a programme, invitation or indeed letters written during wartime.

How Much?

I am often asked how much menus cost to buy and there is no hard and fast rule on this. I suppose the true answer is, how much the seller is asking, and how much the buyer is willing to pay. Prices can vary dramatically, ranging from a few pounds to hundreds of pounds, especially if the menu is signed by a famous person, is well illustrated or commemorates a particularly important occasion. But collecting should be for pleasure, not profit, so it is best to buy what pleases you. That is not to say that menus are not a good investment and if bought wisely will increase in value. Buy the best

you can afford, and in the best condition. I am not suggesting in perfect condition, as many of these menus have been around for a long time and by the nature of the material can easily be damaged.

Rare Menus

Another question I am often asked is: what is a rare menu? That is a very difficult question to answer. When we think of a rare menu card we are thinking of its desirability, its beauty, the date, what it represents, how available it is and, very importantly, how much it costs. These considerations, plus more, constitute what we really mean by the term rare. My main collecting interest has been in royalty, but what is rare to me may not be rare to someone else, and what is rare to someone else may be very common to me. To me, a menu card that is readily available, cheaply, in large numbers cannot be considered as rare. As collections of early menus become fewer, the menus themselves become more collectible. So the term rare is relative to what one collects and what that collector already owns. I like to collect royal menus from the Victorian era for their sheer beauty. The only way I know how to determine whether a menu is rare or not is to spend a few decades collecting, and observing the fluctuations in prices, and trends in the market. Experience is the best teacher, but is not infallible. So when someone asks me for an appraisal of a menu's rarity I consider its condition, age, availability,

subject matter, demand and appeal. All this information comes with experience, and all these criteria help to determine its rarity.

I hope this book gives you many hours of enjoyment, glancing through time at some of the most prestigious banquets and sumptuous meals in history. I know it has given me great pleasure in writing it, renewing some of my own memories, and delving into the lives of the great and the good.

A collection of menus that commemorate various historic occasions over the last century, including New Year's Eve 1939–40 at Quaglino's in London, the Coronation of King George VI in 1937 at the Dorchester (page 50), and the 4th Women's World Games in London on 11 August 1934.

Potage à la Tortue, Consommé Claire, Crême de Riz à la PolonaiseTête

Saumon Mayonnaise, Truite Saumonée Froide, Cailles à la Bordeaux,

à l'Archiduc, Les Poulets Gras au Cresson, Langue de Boeuf Fumée,

Parfait de Foie Gras, Les Epinards aux Croûtons, Jambon de Bayon

d'Oranges, Petits Savarins au Kirsch, Meringues à la Chantilly,

PolonaiseTête de Veau en Tortue, Petite Marmite, Salade de Homard,

à la Bordeaux, Salmis de Gelinottes, Riz de Veau, Filets de Sole Mor

Boeuf Fumée, Suprême de Volaille aux Truffes, Turbot Sauce Hollanda

de Bayonne, Haricots Verts, Filet de Boeuf, Chapon du Mans, Bombe

Bûche de Noël, Potage à la Tortue, Consommé Claire, Crême de Riz

Barquettes d'Ecrevisses, Saumon Mayonnaise, Truite Saumonée Froi

Mornay, Canetons de Rouen à l'Archiduc, Les Poulets Gras au Cress

Hollandaise, Oeufs de Pluviers, Parfait de Foie Gras, Les Epinards au

Mans, Bombe Glacée, Gelée d'Oranges, Petits Savarins au Kirsch,

Crême de Riz à la PolonaiseTête de Veau en Tortue, Petite Marmit

Saumonée Froide, Cailles à la Bordeaux, Salmis de Gelinottes, Riz de V

u Cresson, Langue de Boeuf Fumée, Suprême de Volaille aux Truffes,

ux Croûtons, Jambon de Bayonne, Haricots Verts, Filet de Boeuf, C

Meringues à la Chantilly, Bûche de Noël, Potage à la Tortue, Consomm

Salade de Homard, Barquettes d'Ecrevisses, Saumon Mayonnaise, Trui

Filets de Sole Mornay, Canetons de Rouen à l'Archiduc, Les Poulets

Turbot Sauce Hollandaise, Oeufs de Pluviers, Parfait de Foie Gras, Le

Chapon du Mans, Bombe Glacée, Gelée d'Oranges, Petits Savarins

Consommé Claire, Crême de Riz à la PolonaiseTête de Veau en To

Mayonnaise, Truite Saumonée Froide, Cailles à la Bordeaux, Salm

l'Archiduc, Les Poulets Gras au Cresson, Langue de Boeuf Fumée,

Parfait de Foie Gras, Les Epinards aux Croûtons, Jambon de Bayon

Royal Weddings

Queen Victoria had a large family, and during her long reign there were many wedding breakfasts. These occasions were quite spectacular, and the ornate menus are works of art, with hand-painted borders showing flowers and flags, crests and crowns relating to the royal couple. By modern times the food is much simpler, three or four courses rather than six or seven, and the style of menu is similar to that produced for state banquets, in the form of booklets tied with silk ribbon. Two menus from the Queen's Silver Wedding are shown, the printing of the Crown and Cipher being in silver for the occasion. An unusual royal menu is the one produced for the royal flight which took the Prince and Princess of Wales to Gibraltar for their honeymoon. Finally, two menus, for the wedding and honeymoon of the Duke and Duchess of York, continue the modern theme of simplicity, both of food and design.

A LAVISH CELEBRATION AT WINDSOR CASTLE

PRINCE ALFRED AND THE GRAND DUCHESS MARIE OF RUSSIA

This magnificently illustrated menu is for the banquet held at Windsor Castle to celebrate the marriage of Queen Victoria's son Alfred, Duke of Edinburgh, to the Grand Duchess Marie Alexandrovna Romanov of Russia. Victoria had been keen to marry off the young prince, as he had already got into a scrape in Malta over some lady and London was full of temptations for young men. But when Alfred in 1869 finally set his heart on the lovely young Russian princess Victoria was against the match, claiming that Russia was unfriendly to England and that the Romanovs were arrogant. To make matters worse, after the engagement the Tsar refused to allow Marie to visit Balmoral for the Queen's inspection (Victoria had always interviewed her prospective daughters-in-law). The Tsarina, trying to make amends, then telegraphed Queen Victoria, asking her to travel to Cologne to meet the Russian party there in three days time.

Victoria was outraged, describing the proposal as 'one of the coolest things I ever heard.'

However, in spite of all the ill-feeling the couple were finally married in the chapel of the Winter Palace in St Petersburg on 23 January 1874. It was a romantic, fairy-tale wedding. They then travelled to England to visit the Queen at Windsor, where they received a tremendous welcome from the town. The streets were beautifully decorated with garlands, flowers and flags and packed with well-wishers. Fortunately, Queen Victoria approved of her attractive new daughter-in-law and decided that Marie was going to be a 'treasure' once she had learned English ways. Victoria was determined to make the occasion a great success, as it was the first time she had attended a public banquet since the death of Prince Albert in 1861.

The lavish banquet for 136 guests was held in St George's Hall, the table laid with silver-gilt plate. The huge buffet at the end of the hall was decorated with gold candelabra and other ornaments. The Victorians were hearty eaters and the menu is typical of the period, with five courses and a buffet of roast joints for those who were still hungry after the two soups, thick and clear, the fish, the two meat courses and the desserts. Savarin was often served at these occasions – this is a yeast cake made in a ring mould. The cake is then turned out and soaked in liqueur (kirsch on this occasion) and a fruit sauce.

The elaborately decorated menu to celebrate the marriage of Queen Victoria's son Prince Alfred and the Grand Duchess Marie of Russia, only daughter of the Tsar. At the top it shows two winged cherubs with a shield depicting the arms of the Prince, and the arms of the Romanovs, with the double-headed Imperial eagle.

MENU

Turtle Soup
Clear Vegetable Soup

Boiled Salmon
Fried Fillets of Sole

Chicken Rissoles
Lamb Chops
Chicken Breasts with Truffles
Spiced Fillets of Beef with Madeira Sauce

Roast Chicken
Roast Quail

Asparagus in Sauce

Cake Rings with Kirsch and Apricot Sauce
Orange Jelly
Meringues with Sweetened
Whipped Cream

Buffet
Roast Beef Roast Mutton Roast Venison

Her Majesty's Dinner,

9ᵀᴴ MARCH, 1874.

POTAGES.

A la Tortue ——— A la Julienne.

POISSONS.

Le Saumon bouilli. — Les Filets de Soles frits.

ENTRÉES.

Les Rissolles de Volaille.
Les Côtelettes d'Agneau.
Les Suprême de Poulets aux truffes.
Les Filets de Bœuf piqués, sauce Madère.

RÔTS.

Les Poulets ——— Les Cailles.

ENTREMETS.

Les Asperges à la Sauce.
Les Savarins au Kirsch sauce Abricot.
Le Gelée d'Oranges à l'Anglaise.
Les Meringues à la Chantilly.

BUFFET.

Roast Beef ——— Roast Mutton.
Roast Venison.

THE ROYAL WEDDING BREAKFAST

Thursday 27th April 1882

Potages.

À LA BRUNOISE   À LA CRÊME DE RIZ.

Entrées.

LES COTELETTES D'AGNEAU, PANÉES ET SAUTÉES.
LES FILETS DE POULETS BIGARRÉS AUX TRUFFES.
LES ESCALOPES DE RIS DE VEAU À LA CHICORÉE.
LES FILETS DE CANETONS AUX POIS.

Relevés.

LA PIÈCE DE BOEUF BRAISÉE, SAUCE RAIFORT.
LES POULARDES À LA JARDINIÈRE.

Entrées Froides.

LA SALADE DE HOMARDS.
LES OEUFS DE PLUVIERS.

Rôt.

LES POULETS GRAS AU CRESSON.

Entremêts.

LES POIS SAUTÉS AU BEURRE.
LES ARTICHAUTS À LA LYONNAISE.
LE GATEAU DE GÉNOISE AU CHOCOLAT.
LA CRÈME À LA D'ORLÉANS
LA GELÉE GARNIE D'ORANGES
LA MERINGUE SUISSE À LA CHANTILLY

Relevés

LE PUDDING À LA DIPLOMATE.
LES SOUFFLÉS À LA CANELLE.

QUEEN VICTORIA'S YOUNGEST SON

PRINCE LEOPOLD AND PRINCESS HELENE

An elaborate menu for the wedding breakfast of Prince Leopold to Princess Helene of Waldeck. The arms of the bride and groom are shown, together with their initials and the initials VR, for Queen Victoria.

This highly elaborate menu was produced for the wedding breakfast of Prince Leopold, the youngest son of Queen Victoria, and Princess Helene following their marriage in St George's Chapel, Windsor in April 1882. The pomp and ceremony have a poignant charm now as two years later Leopold was dead, leaving his young wife with a one-year-old daughter and an unborn son.

Leopold had been named after King Leopold of the Belgians, uncle of both Queen Victoria and Prince Albert. While still a baby he was diagnosed as a haemophiliac and spent his childhood as a semi-invalid. Because of his illness a military career was out of the question and so he became a patron of the arts. From 1876 until his death in 1884 he served as the Queen's private secretary.

Princess Helene Frederica was the youngest daughter of the Prince and Princess of Waldeck and Pyrmont, who lived at Darmstadt, in Germany. The Princess of Waldeck was a direct descendant of King George II of Great Britain, and so was related to Queen

Victoria. Leopold was encouraged by Queen Victoria to go to Darmstadt and visit the Waldecks, and so in September 1881 Leopold met Helene for the first time. In November, more meetings were arranged and soon the couple became engaged. They were married the following year, and at the wedding Queen Victoria wore her white wedding veil and lace over her black dress.

She was overjoyed when Helene later gave birth to a girl, who was named Alice after Leopold's beloved sister. The couple set up home at Claremont where they were very happy. Leopold used to drive his daughter around the grounds in a small dogcart, and they had musical evenings when he played the piano. But in March 1884 Leopold died of a brain haemorrhage after a minor fall. Helene gave birth to Leopold's second child in July 1884.

Queen Victoria preferred Windsor to Buckingham Palace, and so both the wedding ceremony and the wedding breakfast took place there. The seven courses were standard for banquets. Some dishes on the menu are unfamiliar to us now: lamb or veal sweetbreads (the thymus gland) were regarded as a delicacy, but with the advent of BSE they are no longer available in Britain; plovers' eggs are now rare and expensive. Diplomat pudding was a favourite at grand occasions: a mould was decorated with crystallized fruit and then filled with alternate layers of sponge fingers soaked in liqueur, a rich egg custard, dried fruit soaked in fruit syrup and apricot jam. It was put on ice to set, then turned out and served with a fruit or liqueur sauce.

MENU

Vegetable Soup Cream of Rice Soup

Lamb Chops in Breadcrumbs, Sautéed
Chicken Fillets with Truffles
Sweetbreads with Chicory
Duck Fillets with Peas

Pot-Roasted Beef with Horseradish Sauce
Chicken with Fresh Vegetables

Lobster Salad
Plovers' Eggs

Chickens with Watercress

Peas in Butter
Artichokes Stuffed with Sausage and Onion

Chocolate Genoa Cake
Custard Cream
Jelly Decorated with Oranges
Swiss Meringue with Sweetened Whipped Cream
Diplomat Pudding
Cinnamon Soufflés

FLORAL TRIBUTES FOR A ROYAL WEDDING

THE DUKE OF YORK AND PRINCESS MARY OF TECK

The future King George V and Queen Mary were married in the Chapel Royal, St James's Palace on 6 July 1893. Queen Victoria wrote of the bride: 'Dear May looked so pretty and quiet and dignified. She was very simply and prettily dressed and wore her Mother's Veil lace'. It was in fact a traditional low-cut court dress in ivory silk satin, with wasp waist and long flounced skirt. Complete with veil and headdress it looked anything but simple.

The menu for the wedding breakfast at Marlborough House has a delicate floral design, showing the white roses of York twined with hawthorn blossom and other flowers that blossom in May, in compliment to the royal bride's name. Her Serene Highness Princess Victoria Mary of Teck was known in her family as May. The daughter of the impoverished Francis, Duke of Teck, she was a

MENU

Bernoise Soup
Cream of Rice Soup

Lamb Chops with Mushrooms
Duck with Peas

Fillets of Beef with Rich Spiced Sauce
Chicken with Watercress

Chicken Mayonnaise
Lobster Salad
Sliced Ham in Aspic
Sliced Tongue in Aspic
Rolled Veal
Foie Gras in Aspic

Green Beans
Spinach

Jellies and Creams
Assorted Pastries

Cold Roast Fowls

great-granddaughter of King George III of Britain. Her mother, Princess Mary Adelaide of Cambridge, known as 'Poor Mary', was a cousin of Queen Victoria. Princess Mary was first engaged in 1891 to George's elder brother Prince Albert, the heir apparent, known as 'Eddy'. But Eddy died of pneumonia in January 1892 when he was only 26. Prince George, known as the Sailor Prince, had meanwhile joined the Royal Navy and was a gunboat commander when his brother died. It was Queen Victoria, George's grandmother, who suggested that he should marry Princess Mary instead. It was very much an arranged marriage – the young couple hardly knew each other – but it was a great success.

The menu is lengthy and elaborate, in the Victorian tradition, and as usual there is a buffet for those who have still not had enough, or who don't care for French menus. What is unusual is that there was no fish course.

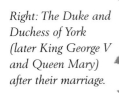

Right: The Duke and Duchess of York (later King George V and Queen Mary) after their marriage.

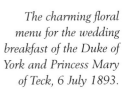

The charming floral menu for the wedding breakfast of the Duke of York and Princess Mary of Teck, 6 July 1893.

THE
ROYAL WEDDING BREAKFAST,
THURSDAY, 6TH JULY, 1893.

POTAGES.
Bernoise à l'Imperatrice.
Crême de Riz à la Polonaise.

ENTRÉES (CHAUDES).
Côtelettes d'Agneau à l'Italienne.
Aiguilettes de Canetons aux Pois.

RELEVÉS.
Filets de Bœuf à la Napolitaine.   Poulets gras au Cresson.

ENTRÉES (FROIDES).
Mayonnaises de Volaille.   Salades d'Homard.
Jambons decoupés à l Aspic.
Langues decoupées à l'Aspic.
Roulardes de Veau.
Pains de Foies à la Gelée.
_____
Haricots Verts.   Les Epinards.
_____
Gelées et Crêmes.
Pâtisserie assortie.
_____
Cold Roast Fowls.

∽ 1972 ∽

HER MAJESTY'S SILVER WEDDING ANNIVERSARY

QUEEN ELIZABETH II AND THE DUKE OF EDINBURGH

Princess Elizabeth walks down the aisle at Westminster Abbey after her marriage in 1947 to Prince Philip, Duke of Edinburgh.

These two menus are from Buckingham Palace. One is for dinner on the Queen's silver wedding day 20 November 1972, and the other is for breakfast on the following day. The Queen and Duke of Edinburgh celebrated 25 years of marriage in 1972 with a service of thanksgiving at Westminster Abbey on 20 November. They then attended a luncheon held in their honour at the Guildhall in the City of London. The dinner in the evening was for family and friends.

During World War II Princess Elizabeth and her sister spent much of their time away from London, living at Balmoral Castle in Scotland or Windsor Castle. It was in 1947 that her engagement was announced to a distant cousin, Lt Philip Mountbatten (formerly Prince Philip of Greece and Denmark). She was then 21.

Their wedding was the first big royal celebration after the end of World War II, and it caused tremendous excitement in the country. Every detail of the wedding dress was pored over – after years of rationing and clothes coupons it was amazing to see such a beautiful dress and such lovely silk fabric. The dress was designed by Norman Hartnell, the couturier. It was made of richly embroidered silk, with garlands of pearl orange blossom, syringa, jasmine and the white rose of York. Princess Margaret, one of the bridesmaids, wore a dress with the same motifs.

After the lavish banquets of her ancestors earlier in this chapter it comes as a surprise to see such a simple menu for a dinner at Buckingham Palace. But the Queen, like her father King George VI, is known to have simple tastes in food. Seven-course dinners with barons of beef, wild boars' heads, stuffed larks and such-likes, are not likely to feature on today's menus.

MENU

Stuffed Eggs

Chicken Breast in a Cream Sauce with Peppers,
Mushrooms and Paprika
Green Beans New Potatoes
Salad

Chocolate Mousse

The Queen said in her speech at the Guildhall luncheon:

I think everybody will concede that on this, of all days, I should begin my speech with the words, 'My husband and I'. I must confess that it came as a bit of a surprise to realize that we had been married twenty-five years. Neither of us is much given to looking back and the years have slipped by so quickly. Now that we have reached this milestone in our lives we can see how immensely lucky we have been, or perhaps fortunate might be a better word. We had the good fortune to grow up in happy and united families, we have been fortunate in our children, and, above all, we are fortunate in being able to serve this great country and Commonwealth. A marriage begins by joining man and wife together, but this relationship between two people, however deep at the time, needs to develop and mature with the passing years.

For that it must be held firm in the web of family relationships, between parents and children, between grandparents and grandchildren, cousins, aunts and uncles. We all know about the difficulties of achieving that Happy Family, but if it succeeds in real life there is nothing like it. A few well chosen words can often say more than volumes. When the Bishop was asked what he thought about sin he replied with simple conviction that he was against it. If I am asked today what I think about family life after twenty-five years I can answer with equal simple conviction. I am for it. It was therefore with a spirit of real thanksgiving for our good fortune that we attended the service in Westminster Abbey this morning, and it is with real pleasure and gratitude that we are here now to receive your congratulations in Guildhall where so many events, great and personal, in the history of Britain and my family, have been celebrated.

MENU

Oeufs Mikardo

———

Suprême de Volaille à la King
Haricots Verts
Pommes Nouvelles
Salade

———

Mousse au Chocolat

WINES
Maximin Grünhäuser Herrenberg 1969
Château Lascombes 1961
Bollinger 1964
Fonseca 1955
Hine, Grande Champagne 1948

Lundi, le 20 Novembre, 1972   BUCKINGHAM PALACE

MENU

———

Salmon Kedgeree

or

Scrambled Egg

Bacon and Mushrooms

Mardi, le 21 Novembre, 1972   BUCKINGHAM PALACE

ROYAL DINING IN THE SKIES

THE PRINCE OF WALES AND LADY DIANA SPENCER

Loyal greetings to

HRH The Prince of Wales and The Lady Diana Spencer

on the occasion of their wedding
at St Paul's Cathedral
on 29th July 1981

British airways

MENU

The wedding of the Prince of Wales and Lady Diana Spencer took place on 29 July 1981. The Concorde menu that day on the flight from London to New York showed pictures of the happy couple beneath the badge of the Prince of Wales – three feathers rising out of a gold coronet.

Concorde was the world's most famous aircraft, a joint Anglo-French enterprise. It went into service in 1976, the inauguration of commercial supersonic travel by the British. The London to Washington service started on 24 May 1976 and proved enormously popular with the rich and famous, captains of industry and movie stars alike. On 8 November 1986 the first round-the-world flight by a British Airways Concorde covered 28,238 miles (45,443km) in 29 hours 59 minutes. But following the accident involving an Air France Concorde outside Paris on 25 July 2000, when everyone on board was killed, British Airways suspended its supersonic operations and Concorde was sadly axed in 2003.

Prince Charles and Lady Diana Spencer were married on 29 July 1981 at St Paul's Cathedral, before an invited congregation of 2,500, including royalty, government leaders and diplomats from around the world. It was the classic fairy-tale wedding, and the whole world, it seemed, came to a halt to watch the proceedings on TV, or at least listen to the commentary on radio. As the

Aperitifs & Cocktails

Sweet and Dry Vermouth
Campari Soda
Americano . Negroni
Medium Dry Sherry
Dry Martini . Gin . Vodka
Bloody Mary . Old Fashioned . Manhattan
Sours – Whisky . Gin . Brandy
Gin Fizz

Highballs – Whisky . Brandy . Gin . Rum

Champagne Cocktail

Spirits

Whisky – Scotch . Bourbon . Rye
Gin
Vodka

Beers

Ale . Lager

Selection of Soft Drinks

Wines

Champagne
Mumm Cordon Rouge 1975

Bordeaux
Château Brane Cantenac 1971
or
Château Cantemerle 1974
as available

White Burgundy
Chablis 1978/79

Liqueurs

Remy Martin Napoleon Brandy
Drambuie . Cointreau
Cockburns Special Reserve Port
or
Fonseca Bin 27
as available

Jamaica Macanudo cigars

Morning Meal

Champagne – Buck's Fizz

Fresh fruit appetizer

Mixed grill
Tournedos of beef wrapped in bacon and grilled
with pork sausages and kidney
or
Coulibiac à la Russe
Scotch salmon cooked in a crust of brioche
pastry with eggs, chopped button mushroom
and rice

Grilled tomato and mushrooms with asparagus spears
and baked straw potatoes

Assorted cheese

Rolls . Croissants

Butter . Preserves

Coffee

bride descended from the Glass Coach at the foot of the steps of St Paul's Cathedral, every detail of the flouncy ivory silk taffeta Emanuel wedding dress was described, as well as the length of the train (25ft/7.5m), the cost of the engagement ring, an 18-carat sapphire surrounded by diamonds, the wedding ring made of Welsh gold, the veil which was made of antique lace and the diamond tiara borrowed from her family. Prince Charles waited for her at the altar flanked by his 'supporters', his brothers Prince Andrew and Prince Edward. It is a royal custom to have supporters rather than a best man.

Up to a million people filled the streets along the wedding procession route from St Paul's Cathedral to Buckingham Palace to cheer the happy couple. Thousands had camped out overnight along the route; fortunately it had been a balmy summer's night. As the couple exchanged vows the roars of the crowds, listening on loudspeakers in the packed London streets, could be heard throughout the cathedral. An estimated 750 million watched worldwide on TV, soaking up the atmosphere, the pomp and circumstance, with the royal family out in force, including the much-loved Queen Mother.

Above left: Concorde in flight.

Far left and above: British Airways menu for the morning meal served on Concorde on the day of the wedding of Prince Charles and Lady Diana.

*Their Royal Highnesses
The Prince and Princess
of Wales*

*

**London — Gibraltar
Saturday 1st August 1981**

Menu for the Royal Flight from London to Gibraltar, 1 August 1981. The newly-weds Prince Charles and Princess Diana took this flight in order to join the Royal Yacht Britannia *for a cruise in the Mediterranean.*

Avocado pear
filled with shredded celery and apple with cottage cheese

* * *

Selection of seafood
Cornish lobster, poached Scotch salmon, Atlantic prawns

* * *

Assorted cold meats
Roast chicken and beef with smoked ham

* * *

Fresh seasonal salad

* * *

Melon fruit cup

* * *

Cheese board - Biscuits

* * *

Coffee

* * *

Petits fours

After the ceremony the couple rode back in the open State Landau to Buckingham Palace for the wedding breakfast, waving to the ecstatic crowds. Later they emerged on the balcony in front of the palace to give the kiss the crowd had been waiting for. It had been a perfect day, and Britons enjoyed a national holiday to mark the occasion.

They then spent three days on honeymoon at the Broadlands estate in Hampshire, the Mountbatten family home, before leaving by Royal Flight for Gibraltar. The Prince and Princess were flown by Squadron Leader D. Lovett, on his last flight in the Royal Air Force after nine years on the Royal Flight, serving from March 1972 to September 1981. Twelve members of the Royal Flight were privileged to attend the wedding, acting as ushers and forming part of the entourage lining the steps of St Paul's Cathedral. At Gibraltar the Royal couple boarded the Royal Yacht *Britannia* for a 12-day cruise through the Mediterranean to Egypt. They then returned to the UK to finish their honeymoon with a stay at Balmoral Castle, always a favourite with Prince Charles.

THE MENUS
It is interesting to compare the two flight menus with the actual wedding breakfast served at Buckingham Palace. The Palace menu consisted of *quenelles* (light fish dumplings) with fish sauce to start with, chicken breast with buttered broad beans, creamed sweetcorn and new potatoes as a main course, salad, and then strawberries and clotted cream as dessert. The menu on the Royal Flight was equally light: stuffed avocado, seafood, cold chicken, beef and ham, salad, melon and cheese. By contrast, the menu served by British Airways on Concorde on the day of the wedding included a mixed grill of beef tournedos, bacon, pork sausage and kidney, followed by salmon in pastry with eggs, mushrooms and rice, and ending with cheese, rolls and croissants – rather a heavy meal for a morning flight in high summer.

The group wedding photograph after the marriage of Prince Charles and Princess Diana. It includes the bride's parents, the Queen and the Duke of Edinburgh, the Queen Mother, Princess Margaret, Princess Anne and her husband, and the princes Andrew and Edward.

A SUMMER WEDDING BREAKFAST

THE DUKE AND DUCHESS OF YORK

The wedding breakfast menu for Prince Andrew and Sarah Ferguson on 23 July 1986 is in striking contrast to the Victorian wedding menus at the beginning of this chapter, with their colourful flags, crowns and coats of arms, the intricate borders and the six or seven courses. The second menu shown (bottom right) is for 28 July, on board the Royal Yacht *Britannia* where they spent their honeymoon, and is equally simple.

Prince Andrew and Sarah Ferguson were married at Westminster Abbey on 23 July 1986. Thousands of people lined the streets of London and a worldwide TV audience of 500 million people tuned in to watch the pageantry.

Sarah Ferguson arrived at the Abbey after riding from Clarence House, the late Queen Mother's residence (now the home of the Prince of Wales) in the famous Glass Coach with her father, Sir Ronald. Inside 2,000 people watched the bride walk up the blue-carpeted aisle, sweeping a 17 feet (5m) train behind her. Prince Edward was best man and Prince Charles read the lesson. Guests included 17 members of foreign royalty, US President Reagan's wife Nancy and Prime Minister Margaret Thatcher.

After the ceremony the couple rode in the open-topped 1902 State Landau to Buckingham Palace, where the wedding breakfast was held. Like his brother Prince Charles, Prince Andrew and his bride spent their honeymoon aboard the Royal Yacht *Britannia*, cruising in the Azores. The menu on the right is for 28 July, five days into their holiday, when they had reached Ponta Delgada.

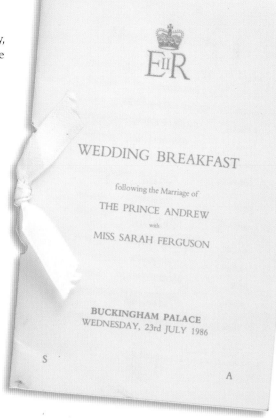

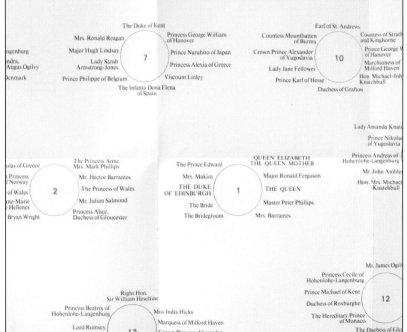

MENU 23 July	MENU 28 July
Stuffed Eggs	Sole in White Wine and Cream, with Grapes
Lamb with Mint Sauce Spinach with Mushrooms Buttered Broad Beans New Potatoes	Fillet of Beef in Mushroom Sauce Cauliflower with Butter Sauce Green Beans Potatoes in Butter
Salad	Salad
Strawberries Clotted Cream	Pineapple Ice

The central tables in the seating plan for the wedding breakfast of Prince Andrew and Miss Sarah Ferguson at Buckingham Palace, 23 July 1981.

Menu

Oeufs Drumkilbo

Carré d'Agneau Paloise
Couronne d'Epinards aux Champignons
Fèves au Beurre
Pommes Nouvelles

Salade

Fraises St. George
Crème Caillée

Les Vins

Piesporter Goldtröpfchen Auslese 1976
Château Langoa Barton 1976
Bollinger 1966
Graham 1966

THE QUEEN
THE DUKE OF EDINBURGH
QUEEN ELIZABETH THE QUEEN MOTHER
THE BRIDE AND BRIDEGROOM

The Prince and Princess of Wales
Prince William of Wales
Prince Henry of Wales
The Prince Edward
The Princess Anne, Mrs. Mark Phillips and
  Captain Mark Phillips
Master Peter Phillips
Miss Zara Phillips
The Princess Margaret, Countess of Snowdon
Viscount Linley
Lady Sarah Armstrong-Jones
Princess Alice, Duchess of Gloucester
The Duke and Duchess of Gloucester
Earl of Ulster
Lady Davina Windsor
Lady Rose Windsor
The Duke and Duchess of Kent
Earl of St. Andrews
Lady Helen Windsor
Prince and Princess Michael of Kent
Lord Frederick Windsor
Lady Gabriella Windsor
Princess Alexandra, the Hon. Mrs. Angus Ogilvy and
  the Hon. Angus Ogilvy
Mr. James Ogilvy
Miss Marina Ogilvy

A relaxed Duke and Duchess of York on board the Royal Yacht Britannia *during their honeymoon cruise.*

MENU

Delice de Sole Veronique

Filet de Boeuf Chasseur
Chou-fleur Hollandaise
Haricots Verts
Pommes Chateau

Salade

Glace aux Ananas

LUNDI, LE 28 JUILLET, 1986   PONTA DELGADA

Potage à la Tortue, Consommé Claire, Crême de Riz à la Polonaise Tête
Saumon Mayonnaise, Truite Saumonée Froide, Cailles à la Bordeaux
l'Archiduc, Les Poulets Gras au Cresson, Langue de Boeuf Fumée,
Parfait de Foie Gras, Les Epinards aux Croûtons, Jambon de Bayon
d'Oranges, Petits Savarins au Kirsch, Meringues à la Chantilly, Bûche
de Veau en Tortue, Petite Marmite, Salade de Homard, Barquettes d'E
Salmis de Gelinottes, Riz de Veau, Filets de Sole Mornay, Canetons
Suprême de Volaille aux Truffes, Turbot Sauce Hollandaise, Oeufs de P
Haricots Verts, Filet de Boeuf, Chapon du Mans, Bombe Glacée, Ge
Noël, Potage à la Tortue, Consommé Claire, Crême de Riz à la Polon
d'Ecrevisses, Saumon Mayonnaise, Truite Saumonée Froide, Cailles à
Canetons de Rouen à l'Archiduc, Les Poulets Gras au Cresson, Langue
Oeufs de Pluviers, Parfait de Foie Gras, Les Epinards aux Croûtons, Ja
Glacée, Gelée d'Oranges, Petits Savarins au Kirsch, Meringues à la Ch
la Polonaise Tête de Veau en Tortue, Petite Marmite, Salade de Hon
Cailles à la Bordeaux, Salmis de Gelinottes, Riz de Veau, Filets de Sole
de Boeuf Fumée, Suprême de Volaille aux Truffes, Turbot Sauce Ho
Jambon de Bayonne, Haricots Verts, Filet de Boeuf, Chapon du Mar
Chantilly, Bûche de Noël, Potage à la Tortue, Consommé Claire, Crê
Homard, Barquettes d'Ecrevisses, Saumon Mayonnaise, Truite Saumo
Sole Mornay, Canetons de Rouen à l'Archiduc, Les Poulets Gras au C
Hollandaise, Oeufs de Pluviers, Parfait de Foie Gras, Les Epinards au
Mans, Bombe Glacée, Gelée d'Oranges, Petits Savarins au Kirsch, M
Crême de Riz à la Polonaise Tête de Veau en Tortue, Petite Marmit
Saumonée Froide, Cailles à la Bordeaux, Salmis de Gelinottes, Riz de V
au Cresson, Langue de Boeuf Fumée, Suprême de Volaille aux Truffes,
aux Croûtons, Jambon de Bayonne, Haricots Verts, Filet de Boeuf, C

Royal Banquets

Royal menus have long been of interest because of the grand banquets held by royalty down the years. The menus of Queen Victoria are particularly elaborate, with a decorative coloured border, and different designs for Balmoral Castle, Osborne House, Windsor Castle and Buckingham Palace. The menus for Victoria's two Jubilee dinners, in 1887 and 1897, are identical in style, though the later one is handwritten. Rather different, with a charming, Pre-Raphaelite feel, is the supper menu for Prince and Princess Christian at Cumberland Lodge in 1885. The 20th-century menus are much plainer in style, and that is true right up to the present day. The sporting menus from Balmoral and Sandringham in the days of Edward VII and George V are quite simple, as are the racing menus produced for royalty at Epsom or Ascot races. The exception is the highly elaborate and decorative menu produced by the Dorchester for the Coronation of George VI in 1937.

VICTORIA'S FAVOURITE DAUGHTER

PRINCESS HELENA AND PRINCE CHRISTIAN OF SCHLESWIG-HOLSTEIN

This menu is for a supper at Cumberland Lodge, the home of Queen Victoria's third daughter Helena and her husband Prince Christian. There is no indication what the occasion was – it almost looks as though it could have been a wedding anniversary, though in fact the couple were married in July 1866.

Princess Helena, known as 'Lenchen', was Victoria's favourite daughter. Victoria wrote of her: 'Poor dear Lenchen, though most useful and active and clever and amiable, does not improve in looks and has great difficulty with her figure and her want of calm, quiet, graceful manners.'

Helena met Prince Christian of Schleswig-Holstein on a trip to Germany with her mother. He was bald, penniless and 13 years older than her, but the young princess saw him as her only chance of escape. Resigned to losing Lenchen as a companion, Victoria gave her consent to the marriage, but only if the prospective groom agreed to live at Frogmore, in the grounds of Windsor Castle. Her first two daughters had German husbands, and Victoria was determined not to lose another daughter abroad. Prince Christian, impoverished and with no occupation, was happy to accept, and so they were married in the private chapel in Windsor Castle in July 1866.

The couple lived first at Frogmore and then later at Cumberland Lodge, Windsor, where Christian was given the job of Ranger of Windsor Castle Park. They had six children of whom only four survived.

The supper menu mainly consists of cold dishes and is typically heavy, though the guests would have had dinner earlier. *Pralines* are a very delicate sweet, consisting of almonds covered with a coating of caramelized sugar, said to have been invented by the duc de Choiseul-Pralin.

Princess Helena Augusta Victoria, third daughter of Queen Victoria, and Prince Christian of Schleswig-Holstein at the time of their engagement in 1865.

```
MENU
Clear Soup
Puréed Chicken Soup

Lobster Salad
Chicken Mayonnaise
Chicken in Aspic
Boned and Stuffed Chicken in Aspic
Plovers' Eggs
Sliced Ham
Chicken
Tongue

Genoese Cake with Orange Icing
Little Cake Rings with Kirsch
Warm Sugared Almonds
Chocolate Cakes
Orange Jelly
Champagne Jelly with Chopped Fruit
Coffee Creams
Vanilla Creams
```

Cumberland Lodge.

Souper du 18 Mai, 1885.

Potages.

Consommé Claire.
Purée à la Reine.

Salades de Homards.
Mayonaises de Poulets.
Poulards à l'Aspic.
Galantines à la Gelée.
Oeufs de Pluviers.
Jambons de Conpés.
Poulets. Langues.

Genoises Glacés à l'Orange.
Petits Savarins au Kirsch.
Chaux Pralines au Amandes.
Gâteaux Ambroisie au Chocolat.
Geleés Macedoine au Champagne.
Gelées d'Oranges rubannees.
Crêmes au Câfe.
Crêmes à la Vanille.

OSBORNE

Her Majesty's Dinner

Christmas Day 1895.

Potages.

La Tête de Veau en Tortue.   Au Riz clair

Poissons.

Le Turbot sauce Hollandaise.

Les Filets de Soles frits.

Entrée.

Les Kromeskys de Homard.

Relevé.

Le Dinde à la Chipolata

Chine of Pork.

Entremêts.

Les Asperges à la sauce.

Mince Pies.

Plum Pudding'

Les Eclairs au Chocolat.

Side Table.

Baron of Beef.   Boars Head.   Woodcock Pie.   Game Pie

Brawn.

Hot Roast Beef.

ROYAL CHRISTMAS AT OSBORNE HOUSE

QUEEN VICTORIA AND THE ROYAL FAMILY

Her Majesty's Dinner for Queen Victoria at Osborne, 25 December 1895, was a very grand affair, with six courses, including a buffet of hot and cold dishes.

Osborne House on the Isle of Wight was the private residence of the Queen. She was invariably at Osborne during the yachting season and at Christmas, when she delighted in surrounding herself with her children and grandchildren.

Victoria and Albert had bought Osborne House early in their marriage, and spent many happy times there, sketching, writing and making improvements to the park. The Queen could sit on the beach in her beach-hut, designed by Prince Albert, and watch the ships sail out from Portsmouth, and she also delighted to bathe in the sea, using a bathing-machine. This contraption was pulled right into the water. The Queen, in a voluminous bathing-dress, then stepped out on to the verandah, concealed with curtains, and went down the steps into the sea. She called Osborne her 'little Paradise'.

MENU

Clear Rice Soup
Mock-Turtle Soup

Turbot with Butter Sauce
Fried Fillets of Sole

Lobster Croquettes

Turkey with Chipolatas
Loin of Pork

Asparagus with Sauce

Mince Pies
Plum Pudding
Chocolate Eclairs

Buffet
Baron of Beef, Boar's Head, Game Pie,
Brawn, Hot Roast Beef

She also spent some time there after Prince Albert's death, where she sought solace from her grief, and it was there she died peacefully in 1901.

It was the German-born Prince Albert who introduced many of the customs we now associate with Christmas: the evergreen tree with lights (candles were used before the invention of electric lights), the presents under the tree, and even the decorating of rooms with evergreen boughs.

The menu is typically Victorian, with its long list of heavy dishes. The veal soup *en tortue* is also known as mock-turtle soup, and was very popular at the time, as was real turtle soup. Mock-turtle is made with a calf's head, boned and cooked in stock. The soup is strained and served with small pieces of the meat. Lobster Kromeskys are a kind of croquette, made with diced lobster in white sauce. The lobster pieces are wrapped in caul (pig's membrane), dipped in batter and deep fried. Plum pudding is the old name for Christmas pudding. The dishes on the buffet, usually hearty English fare such as roast beef, were always in English on the menu.

Left: Menu design for Osborne, 1895, surmounted by the royal coat of arms, with the entwined initials VR, ie Victoria Regina (Queen) at either side.

Queen Victoria at Osborne House in 1896, surrounded by children and grandchildren.

GOLDEN AND DIAMOND JUBILEES

QUEEN VICTORIA'S TRIUMPH

The first menu illustrated is for the banquet held on 21 June 1887, the second day of Queen Victoria's Golden Jubilee celebrations, marking 50 years of her reign.

On 20 June the day began quietly with breakfast under the trees at Frogmore, the resting place of her beloved Prince Albert. She then travelled by train from Windsor to Paddington and across the park to Buckingham Palace for a royal banquet in the evening. Fifty foreign kings and princes, along with the governing heads of Britain's overseas colonies and dominions, attended the feast. She wrote in her diary of the event: 'All the Royal personages assembled in the Bow Room and we dined in the Supper-room, which looked splendid with the buffet covered with the gold plate . . .The King of Denmark took me in, and Willy of Greece sat on my other side. The Princes were all in uniform, and the Princesses were all beautifully dressed.'

On the following day, Queen Victoria travelled in an open carriage to Westminster Abbey for a thanksgiving service, escorted by

Official Diamond Jubilee portrait of Queen Victoria 1897.

Indian cavalry. The procession through London, according to Mark Twain, 'stretched to the limit of sight in both directions'. She refused to wear a crown, wearing instead her usual bonnet, though it was a very special one, decorated with diamonds and lace. In the evening, she wore a splendid gown embroidered with silver roses, thistles and shamrocks for the banquet. Afterwards she received a long procession of diplomats and Indian princes until 'half dead with fatigue'. She was then wheeled in her chair to the Chinese Room to sit and watch the fireworks in the garden. It had been a long day.

The menu on this very special occasion was for six courses, with the usual buffet of cold meats. The sole dish is very elaborate: the fillets of sole are spread with a stuffing of whiting mixed with breadcrumbs, herbs and beaten eggs, folded in two, coated in egg and breadcrumbs and cooked in butter. The fillets are then arranged in a circle, alternating with little poached shapes of whiting stuffing, and sprinkled with brown butter. The centre of the dish is filled with shrimps, mushrooms and truffles in a cream fish sauce flavoured with Madeira. The chicken dish is equally spectacular, garnished with cocks' combs, cocks' kidneys, tiny dumplings, lambs' sweetbreads, mushrooms, olives and sliced truffles. One of the sweets is in German: *Sprütz Gebackenes*. We don't know what it was, but of course the German connection is strong: Prince Albert was German, several of Victoria's children had married Germans, and visiting Germany frequently, they would be familiar with German food.

DIAMOND JUBILEE

The second menu marks a banquet held on 23 June after the celebrations for Queen Victoria's Diamond Jubilee, ten years later. Sunday 20 June was the actual anniversary of her accession, and there was a special family thanksgiving service in St George's Chapel, Windsor. Similar Jubilee services were held at 11 o'clock in every church, chapel and synagogue in the country.

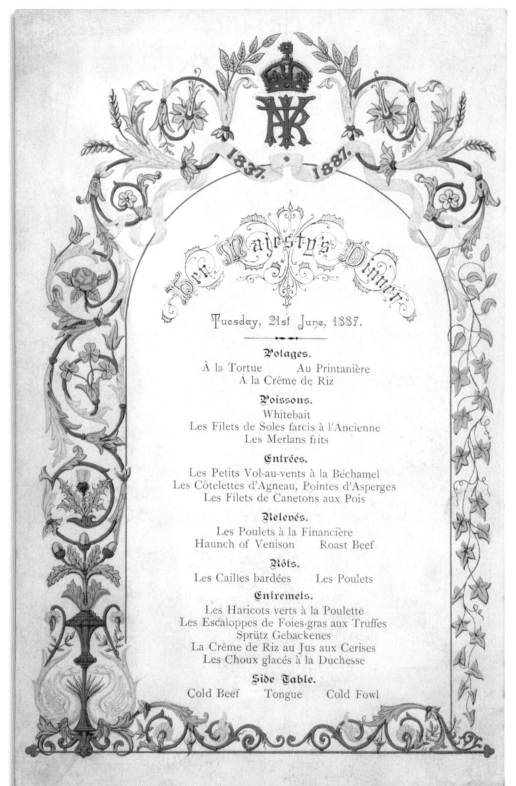

Her Majesty's Dinner

Tuesday, 21st June, 1887.

Potages.
À la Tortue   Au Printanière
À la Crême de Riz

Poissons.
Whitebait
Les Filets de Soles farcis à l'Ancienne
Les Merlans frits

Entrées.
Les Petits Vol-au-vents à la Béchamel
Les Côtelettes d'Agneau, Pointes d'Asperges
Les Filets de Canetons aux Pois

Relevés.
Les Poulets à la Financière
Haunch of Venison   Roast Beef

Rôts.
Les Cailles bardées   Les Poulets

Entremets.
Les Haricots verts à la Poulette
Les Escaloppes de Foies-gras aux Truffes
Sprütz Gebackenes
La Crême de Riz au Jus aux Cerises
Les Choux glacés à la Duchesse

Side Table.
Cold Beef   Tongue   Cold Fowl

GOLDEN JUBILEE MENU

Turtle Soup
Cream of Rice Soup
Vegetable Soup

Whitebait
Fillets of Sole, Stuffed and
Garnished with a Cream Sauce of
Shrimps, Mushrooms and Truffles
Fried Whiting

Vol-au-Vents with White Sauce
Lamb Chops with
Asparagus Tips
Duckling with Peas

Chicken Garnished with Cocks'
Combs, Cocks' Kidneys,
Dumplings, Sweetbreads,
Mushrooms, Olives and Truffles
Haunch of Venison
Roast Beef

Roast Quail
Roast Chicken

Green Beans in Cream Sauce
Garnished with Onions and
Mushrooms
Sliced Foie Gras with Truffles

Sprütz Gebackenes
Cream Rice with Cherry Juice
Iced Puff Pastries

Side Table
Cold Beef, Tongue, Cold Chicken

Menu for the banquet held on 21 June 1887, on the occasion of Queen Victoria's Golden Jubilee.

For the official celebrations, Victoria travelled to Paddington by royal train. Instead of the Crowned Heads of Europe, the dignitaries invited this time were the Colonial Premiers of the British Empire. On 22 June Victoria made a grand procession through London in an open carriage, pausing outside St Paul's Cathedral for a short service of thanksgiving, as she was too lame to climb the steps. The procession was a triumph, London sparkling with gas lights and the newfangled electric light bulbs. The Queen's progress continued via the Mansion House across London Bridge and through South London, before returning over Westminster Bridge, past the Houses of Parliament to Buckingham Palace. In her Journal the Queen wrote: 'No one ever, I believe, has met with such an ovation as was given to me, passing through those six miles of streets . . . The cheering was quite deafening and every face seemed to be filled with real joy.'

Her Majesty's Dinner
Wednesday 23rd June 1897

Potages
A la Purée d'Asperges
Au Hochepot de poulets
Poissons
Le Turbot S.ce Hollandaise
Les filets de soles à la Maréchale
Entrées
Les Mousses à la Régence
Le Chaud froid à la S.t Lambert
Rôt —
Les Canetons
Entremêts
Les Epinards aux Croûtons
Le Pouding à la Princesse
Les petits soufflés à la Pompadour
Side Table
Hot & Cold Fowl. Tongue. Hot & Cold Beef

The hand-written menu for the Diamond Jubilee dinner on the 23 June has six courses and thirteen dishes. The entrées were very elaborate: chicken mousse garnished with sliced lamb's sweetbreads, truffles in Madeira, chicken dumplings, cock's combs and prawns, and cold poached chicken, coated with an egg cream sauce and aspic.

Handwritten menu for the banquet at Buckingham Palace on 23 June 1897 to celebrate Queen Victoria's Diamond Jubilee.

Queen Victoria's Diamond Jubilee procession passes the Mansion House in London, watched by cheering, waving crowds.

AN ANGLO-FRENCH OCCASION

BANQUET GIVEN FOR KING EDWARD VII BY PRESIDENT LOUBET OF FRANCE

The menu for this magnificent banquet given for King Edward VII in 1903 is printed on silk. On one side is a portrait of the King by W. & D. Downey of London, and on the other side the menu.

While still Prince of Wales, Edward had travelled extensively in Europe, and he spoke French fluently. This made him a good ambassador in foreign relations and his forays into foreign policy had a direct bearing on Anglo-French relations. The idea for the Entente Cordiale sprang from a meeting between the Prince of Wales and the French statesman Léon Gambetta in 1881. After he became King in 1901 Edward promoted the idea and so an agreement was negotiated between the French and British Foreign Secretaries.

This was one of King Edward's most important foreign trips: an official visit to France in May 1903 as the guest of President Émile Loubet at the Élysée Palace. This visit helped create the atmosphere for the Entente Cordiale, an informal agreement regarding the various British and French colonies in North Africa and acknowledging the right of free passage through the Suez Canal and the Straits of Gibraltar.

Signed by the French Ambassador Paul Cambon and the British Foreign Secretary Lord Lansdowne on 8 April 1904, the Entente marked the end of centuries of Anglo-French rivalry and Britain's 'splendid isolation' from continental affairs. It also paved the way for the diplomatic and military cooperation between the two countries in the run-up to World War I.

By permission of W. D Downey. London

This is a very grand menu for a very special occasion. The soups are very English, especially Windsor Soup, a hearty beef broth, but the other dishes are haute cuisine. The French have pulled out all the stops here, with such dishes as suckling lamb from Pauillac, renowned for its flavour, hazel grouse, which has a strong 'woody' flavour, and Rouen duckling, also considered the best. Foie gras (specially fattened goose liver), one of the famous delicacies, is served cooked with brandy and truffles. The chicken dish also includes truffles, with their incomparable musky perfume. The salad is garnished with cocks' combs while the asparagus is the prized Argenteuil variety, served with butter sauce enriched with whipped cream.

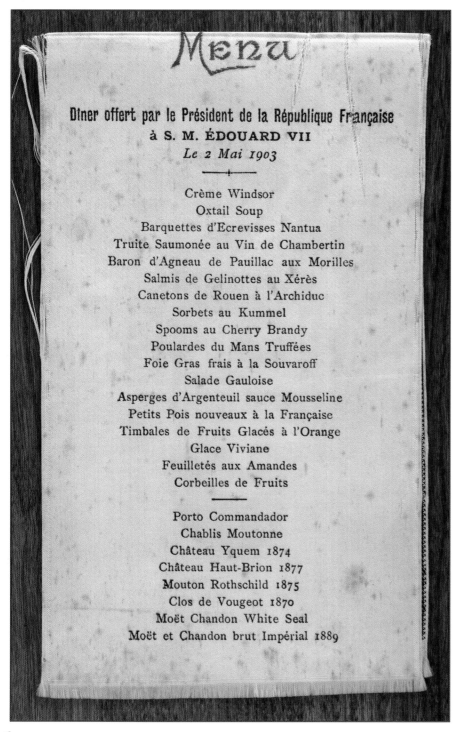

Menu

Diner offert par le Président de la République Française
à S. M. ÉDOUARD VII
Le 2 Mai 1903

Crème Windsor
Oxtail Soup
Barquettes d'Ecrevisses Nantua
Truite Saumonée au Vin de Chambertin
Baron d'Agneau de Pauillac aux Morilles
Salmis de Gelinottes au Xérès
Canetons de Rouen à l'Archiduc
Sorbets au Kummel
Spooms au Cherry Brandy
Poulardes du Mans Truffées
Foie Gras frais à la Souvaroff
Salade Gauloise
Asperges d'Argenteuil sauce Mousseline
Petits Pois nouveaux à la Française
Timbales de Fruits Glacés à l'Orange
Glace Viviane
Feuilletés aux Amandes
Corbeilles de Fruits

Porto Commandador
Chablis Moutonne
Château Yquem 1874
Château Haut-Brion 1877
Mouton Rothschild 1875
Clos de Vougeot 1870
Moët Chandon White Seal
Moët et Chandon brut Impérial 1889

MENU
Windsor Soup
Oxtail Soup

Crayfish Tartlets in Cream Sauce
Salmon Trout in Wine
Baron of Suckling Lamb with Morel
Mushrooms
Braised Hazel Grouse with Sherry
Rouen Ducklings in Cream Sauce

Sorbet with Kummel
Sherbet Meringue with Cherry Brandy

Chicken with Truffles
Foie Gras with Brandy and Truffles
Salad Garnished with Cocks' Combs
and Kidneys

Asparagus with Cream Sauce
New Peas Braised with Lettuce and Onions

Mould of Glacé Fruits with Orange Sauce
Ice Cream Viviane
Pastries with Almonds
Basket of Fruit

Menu, printed on silk, for the sumptuous dinner served at the Élysée Palace, Paris, in honour of King Edward VII, a noted gourmet and bon viveur.

A ROYAL SHOOTING PARTY AT SANDRINGHAM
KING EDWARD VII

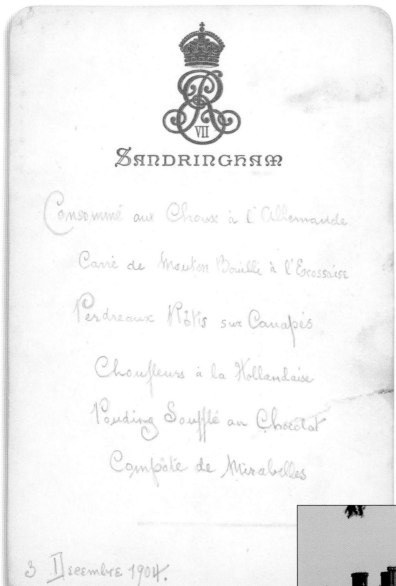

Above: Menu for a shooting party on 3 December 1904 at Sandringham House.

Sandringham House in Norfolk, the country house bought for the Prince of Wales in 1862 by Queen Victoria.

This shooting lunch menu from Sandringham House in Norfolk on 3 December 1904 is fairly simple, as royal meals go. The dishes for these lunches were kept in a hot box made to King Edward's specification, with compartments for storing hot dishes for up to 30 or 40 guests. The box of food, with wines, spirits and anything else required, would be brought out to the shooting lodge by pony and trap and set out either indoors, or on trestle tables outside if the weather was fine. The ladies of the party sometimes came out by coach or trap on these occasions to join the sportsmen for lunch.

Sandringham House was bought for Edward, Prince of Wales, by Queen Victoria because she wanted him to have a private residence away from his official London home, Marlborough House. Here he could escape from society, she thought, and enjoy the benefits of a healthy country life, away from all the temptations of London, including the ladies.

MENU

Game and Cabbage Soup

Boiled Mutton Ribs
Roast Partridge, served on toast

Cauliflower with Butter Sauce

Chocolate Soufflé
Stewed Plums

Sandringham had been owned by the Hon. Charles Spencer Cowper, a stepson of the Prime Minister, Lord Palmerston. When he decided to sell his house in 1862 the Prince of Wales went to see it and liked it. The Queen agreed and the purchase was concluded. Lodges had to be built in the grounds to accommodate the household, guests and members of staff. In 1891 a fire broke out while the house was being prepared for the Prince's 50th birthday. Many rooms were badly damaged, but the Prince decided to go ahead with his birthday celebration, erecting a temporary roof.

Shooting parties were very popular in those days. House parties of friends would be invited for a long weekend, to enjoy hunting, shooting and fishing. In the evenings they would be entertained with music, parlour games and elaborate dinners. On becoming king, Edward hosted many shooting parties for his friends at Sandringham, with 12-course dinners that lasted for hours. The King and his party would retire some time after midnight, before which a further meal, supper, was served. His nickname, obviously very apt, was Tum Tum.

The menu is simple but substantial, with game soup, boiled mutton and roast partridge, cauliflower in white sauce and puddings. *Mirabelles* are a French variety of small yellow plums with a delicious sweet flavour.

Edward, Prince of Wales, with friends on a shooting party.

Lily Langtry, one of King Edward's mistresses, in her theatrical debut in She Stoops to Conquer *at London's Haymarket Theatre, 1881.*

SIMPLE FARE AT BALMORAL CASTLE
KING GEORGE V

The tastes of King George V were much simpler than his father, King Edward VII, as is shown in the menu illustrated from Balmoral Castle for 26 August 1922.

However, Queen Mary took charge of the entertaining and maintained a high standard at banquets and parties, dealing directly with the chef, for if left to the King the menus on these occasions would have been plain and simple.

Balmoral, situated in Aberdeenshire, in the north-east of Scotland, was first known as a royal residence in the 14th century, when King Robert II of Scotland used a hunting lodge there. Queen Victoria and Prince Albert first rented Balmoral in 1848, Victoria describing it as a 'pretty little castle'. They liked it so much that when the owner died they decided to buy it. They commissioned a new house, in Victorian baronial style, which became the present Balmoral Castle. Prince Albert planned the grounds and was involved in the plans for the house, which was completed in 1856. The décor was described by one visitor as suffering from 'tartanitis'. Prince Albert took to wearing a kilt, while Victoria chose a dress in tartan satin. After the death of Prince Albert, Victoria enjoyed the peace and seclusion in the company of her faithful gillie John Brown.

King George V equally enjoyed Balmoral, being a keen huntsman and fisherman, and the castle remains a favourite with the royal family. Prince Charles, a skilled watercolour artist, has painted some charming views of Balmoral and its surroundings.

With the outbreak of World War I in 1914 food shortages came to the royal household, and there were a number of restrictions on food. Meat was only served three times a week and only at dinner, for the royal family and the royal household. The King was very fond of curry, a taste he had developed in India, but this was

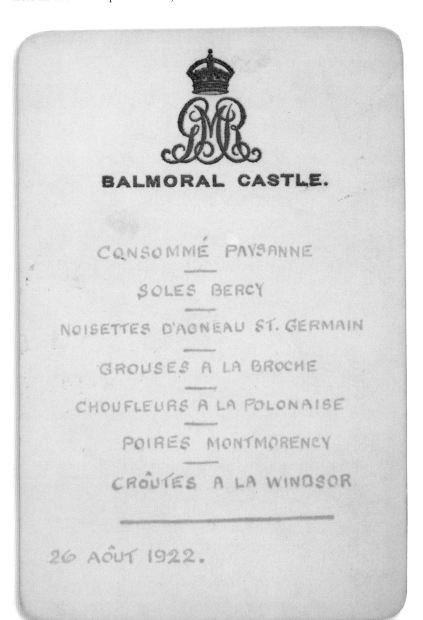

MENU

Clear Vegetable Soup

Sole in White Wine Sauce

Sautéed Lamb Fillet, served on Toast with Veal Stock and Purée of Peas

Spit-Roast Grouse

Cauliflower Served with Chopped Hard-Boiled Egg

Pears with Cherry Ice Cream

Savouries

served only at private meals. He also insisted on his favourite, mashed potatoes, being served at private meals.

The menu shown here for 1922 is very plain and simple in contrast to the Victorian and Edwardian examples, though still written in French and still containing several courses. The shooting season opens on 12 August, so the King, a keen shot, may even have shot the grouse himself.

Balmoral Castle, in Aberdeenshire, Scotland, one of Queen Victoria's favourite homes.

GEORGE V AND WORLD WAR I

World War I caused a lot of difficulties for the royal family, not least because the Kaiser, Wilhelm II, was a cousin of George V. Because of the high anti-German feeling during the war the royal family finally changed their name from Saxe-Coburg-Gotha to Windsor. The new name was adopted by a royal proclamation of George V in 1917.

During the war King George made over 450 visits to troops and over 300 visits to hospitals, visiting wounded servicemen. He also pressed for better treatment of prisoners-of-war, and more humane treatment of conscientious objectors, some of whom were sent to labour camps or forced into the army against their will.

King George V shooting at Balmoral.

THE SPORT OF KINGS

KING EDWARD VII AND KING GEORGE V AT ASCOT AND EPSOM RACES

Edward VII loved everything about horse-racing and was a familiar figure at race meetings. This menu for the royal party at Epsom Downs June 1907 is typical of the period.

As Prince of Wales his horse Persimmon, ridden by the jockey John Watts, won the Derby in 1896. A bronze statue of the horse stands in front of the stables at Sandringham. He won again in 1900 with Diamond Jubilee, this time with Herbert Jones as the jockey, and a third time in 1909 with Minoru, also ridden by Herbert Jones. He used the prize money to improve his estate at Sandringham, adding walled gardens, pergolas and greenhouses growing exotic fruit. Queen Victoria disapproved of Prince Edward's interest in horse-racing and theatre-going, and it was to keep him away from such activities that she had bought Sandringham House for him.

The Prince of Wales Stakes, named after him, was first run at Royal Ascot in 1862. He was such a well-loved figure at the races that the Ascot race meeting in June 1910, following his death the previous May, was known as Black Ascot, as everyone wore mourning, including stylish black dresses, in honour of his memory.

The menu for the 1907 Epsom race meeting is not so colourful or elaborate in design as Victorian menus, but the food is equally rich and lavish, including lobster, quail, plovers' eggs and asparagus. King Edward loved his food as much as he loved racing.

EPSOM.

Mayonnaise de Homard.
Filets de Soles à la Valenciennes.

———

Chaufroix de Volaille à l'Indienne.
Cailles Nappées à la Demidoff.

———

Derby Beef.	Roast Beef.
Jambon d'York.	Agneau, Sauce Menthe.
Poulardes Froides.	Langue à l'Ecarlate.
Galantine de Volaille.	Pressed Beef.

———

Œufs de Pluviers.
Asperges Froides.　　Salade de Romaine.

———

Macédoine de Fruits.　　Tarte de Groseilles Vertes.
Savarins au Chocolat.　　Pâtisseries Parisienne.

———

Dessert.

4 *Juin*, 1907.

Above left: The bronze statue of the Prince of Wales horse Persimmon, which won the Derby in 1896.

Above and right: Royal menus for race meetings at Epsom 1907 and Ascot 1935.

The menu for Royal Ascot on 19 June 1935, although some 28 years later, has similar food on offer, the differences being salmon and mutton pies, with Eton mess and cakes to end the meal. Eton mess, traditionally served at Eton College on 4 June, is a mixture of chopped strawberries, sugar, crumbled meringues, whipped cream and kirsch.

Racing first took place at East Cote, as it was originally known, in 1711, when Queen Anne decided it was an ideal place for 'horses to stretch'. Ascot has retained close links with the royal family ever since, and Royal Ascot is the only true royal racing event in the world. Royal Ascot is the epitome of style and sophistication, the tone being set in Edwardian times when the Prince of Wales, later King Edward VII, was a keen race-goer. With his flamboyant life-style and his mistresses, including Lily Langtry and Alice Keppel, he dominated the racing scene in his lifetime.

Edward's son King George V, although not a passionate racing monarch like his father, won the 1000 Guineas in 1928 with his horse Scuttle, his only classic success.

The Ascot race meeting in June 1910 following King Edward's death was known as Black Ascot, as all the racegoers wore mourning in honour of his memory.

Rosettes de Saumon au Rubis

———

Côtelettes d'Agneau Argenteuil
Poulet en Chaud-froid à l' Indienne
Cailles en Aspic Richelieu
Petits Pâtés de Mouton à la Windsor

———

Pois à la Française et Pommes nouvelles

———

BUFFET { Roast Beef, Derby Beef, Jambon, Langue, Pâté de Poulet

———

Salade White Ladye

———

Eton Mess et Biscuits
Petits Gâteaux

———

Gâteau Sablaise et Genoise nature

ASCOT   19 JUIN, 1935

MENU EPSOM 1907	MENU ASCOT 1935
Lobster Mayonnaise	Salmon Rosettes
Fillets of Sole with Rice	
	Lamb Chops with Asparagus
Cold Poached Chicken with	Cold Poached Chicken in Curry
Curry Sauce	Sauce
Quail with Madeira Sauce and	Quail in Aspic, Garnished with
Truffles	Stuffed Tomatoes and
	Mushrooms
Derby Beef Roast Beef	Mutton Pies
York Ham Lamb with Mint	
Sauce	Peas Braised with Lettuce and
Cold Chicken Pickled Tongue	Onions and New Potatoes
Poached Chicken, Boned and	
Stuffed	Roast Beef, Derby Beef, Ham,
Pressed Beef	Tongue, Chicken Pie
Plovers' Eggs	Salad
Cold Asparagus	
Salad	Eton Mess and Biscuits
	Little Cakes
Chilled Fruit Salad	
Gooseberry Tart	Shortbread and Genoa Cake
Chocolate Cake Rings	
French Pastries	

IN CELEBRATION OF THE CORONATION

BUCKINGHAM PALACE, THE DORCHESTER, LONDON, AND THE WALDORF-ASTORIA, NEW YORK

We have here three menus for dinners given in celebration of the Coronation of King George VI. The one on this page is for the dinner given by the King and Queen at Buckingham Palace the day after the Coronation, 13 May 1937. On the two following pages are the menus for dinners on the actual day of the Coronation, 12 May, one at the Dorchester Hotel, London, and one at the Waldorf-Astoria, New York.

King George had never expected to be king. He was the second son of George V, christened Prince Albert Frederick Arthur George and known in the family as Bertie. His elder brother, the popular Prince Edward, was ahead of him in the line of succession.

He attended Dartmouth Naval College and then joined the Royal Navy. He served in the Navy during World War I, serving on HMS *Collingwood* at the battle of Jutland.

After the war he was created Duke of York and carried out public duties for his father, but his severe stammer made public life an ordeal. As a second son he was allowed some freedom in his choice of wife, marrying Elizabeth Bowes-Lyon in 1923.

King George V died on 20 January 1936 and Prince Edward (known as David by his family) succeeded to the throne. He had developed a relationship with an American divorcée Wallis Simpson,

BUCKINGHAM PALACE.

Tortue Claire de Terrapène
—
Délices de Soles Reine Mary
—
Cailles en Aspic Georges VI
—
Selles d'Agneau à l'Anglaise
Petits Pois au beurre et Pommes Nouvelles
—
Poulets de Printemps rôtis
Salade Mimosa
Asperges, Sauce Mousseuse
—
Soufflés glacés Reine Elizabeth
Corbeilles de Friandises
—
Sablées au Chester

13 Mai, 1937

MENU

Clear Terrapin Soup

Fillets of Sole

Quail in Aspic

Saddle of Lamb, with
Carrots and Onions
Peas in Butter
New Potatoes

Spring Chicken, Roasted
Mixed Salad Sprinkled with
Chopped Hard-Boiled Egg
Asparagus with Cream
Sauce

Glazed Soufflés
Basket of Sweetmeats

Cheese Straws

---

whom he wished to marry, and after becoming King this was reported in the foreign (but not the UK) press. Pressure was put on him by the Prime Minister and the Archbishop of Canterbury, and he was made aware that his decision to marry Wallis would be unpopular with the public. On 10 December 1936 King Edward VIII abdicated, to the dismay of his brother Bertie, who would now succeed to the throne.

The Coronation menus of Buckingham Palace and the Dorchester Hotel have a certain

Above: Dinner menu at Buckingham Palace 13 May 1937.

Cover of the Coronation Dinner menu at the Dorchester, 12 May 1937. It has many references to the British Empire.

King George VI and Queen Elizabeth on the balcony of Buckingham Palace after the Coronation in 1937, with Princess Elizabeth, Princess Margaret and his mother Queen Mary.

similarity: they are both long, seven and six courses respectively, but the dishes are light, with only one soup, turtle, and one fish dish, sole. The turtle soup at Buckingham Palace is made with terrapin, a small American turtle. There are none of the turbots, wild boar's heads, barons of beef or heavy puddings of their ancestors, though Buckingham Palace does have saddle of lamb. Both finish with glazed soufflé, with sweetmeats at the Palace and strawberries at the Dorchester.

The English-Speaking Union was founded in the US in 1920, two years after its establishment in the British Commonwealth. It was conceived as a nonpolitical association dedicated to furthering friendship and understanding among English-speaking peoples around the world. Their Coronation menu at the Waldorf-Astoria also has seven courses, but again the feel is light and elegant. The cocky leeky soup is a traditional Scottish soup, cock-a-leekie, made with chicken and leeks. The kernel of lamb is presumably a round fillet of lamb, sautéed.

Below: Dinner menu at the Dorchester Hotel, London, 12 May 1937.

Menu

Les Perles Ambrées de Sterlet

Le Fumet de Tortue des Îles au Xérès

Les Délices de Sole Jumelés Queen Mary

Le Friand d'Agnelet George VI
La Timbale de Petits Pois Frais
Les Pommes Mignonnettes

Le Blanc de Volaille Givré Elizabeth
Les Reines de Lauris au Citron

Le Soufflé Glacé Empire
Les Fraises des Bois Margaret Rose
Les Excellences Royales

BANQUET
OF
ENGLISH-SPEAKING UNION
OF THE UNITED STATES

IN CELEBRATION OF THE

CORONATION
OF
THEIR MAJESTIES
KING GEORGE VI and QUEEN ELIZABETH

THE WALDORF-ASTORIA
WEDNESDAY, MAY TWELFTH
1937

Menu

CHILLED SUPREME OF HONEYDEW MELON
WITH FRESH BLUEBERRIES

🌢

COCKY LEEKY SOUP

🌢

HEARTS OF CELERY   RIPE & GREEN OLIVES
SALTED ALMONDS & CASHEW NUTS

🌢

COLD SALMON TROUT IN JELLY
CORONATION SAUCE

🌢

KERNEL OF BERKSHIRE LAMB
MINT FLAVORED NEW GREEN PEAS
DEVONSHIRE POTATOES

🌢

MAYTIME SALAD

🌢

CROWN OF VANILLA ICE CREAM
WITH FRESH STRAWBERRIES
FANCY CAKES

🌢

DEMI TASSE

Program

DR. JOHN H. FINLEY
President, New York Branch, English-Speaking Union
Presiding

INVOCATION
DR. J. S. BONNELL
Fifth Avenue Presbyterian Church

HONORABLE JOHN W. DAVIS
President, English-Speaking Union of the United States
will propose the Toasts

ADDRESS
THE RIGHT REVEREND JAMES DE WOLF PERRY
Bishop of Rhode Island and Presiding Bishop of the
Protestant Episcopal Church in America

SOLO
MARGARET HALSTEAD
Dramatic Soprano of the Metropolitan Opera Company
"Land of Hope and Glory", Elgar

ADDRESS
SIR GERALD CAMPBELL, K.C.M.G.
His Britannic Majesty's Consul General in New York

MR. NORMAN COKE-JEPHCOTT at the organ.

*Dinner menu at the Waldorf-Astoria
Hotel, New York, 12 May 1937.*

Potage à la Tortue, Consommé Claire, Crême de Riz à la PolonaiseTête de Veau en Tortue, Petite Marmite, Salade de Homard, Barquettes d'Ecrevisses, Saumon Mayonnaise, Truite Saumonée Froide, Cailles à la Bordeaux, Salmis de Gelinottes, Riz de Veau, Filets de Sole Mornay, Canetons de Rouen à l'Archiduc, Les Poulets Gras au Cresson, Langue de Boeuf Fumée, Suprême de Volaille aux Truffes, Turbot Sauce Hollandaise, Oeufs de Pluviers, Parfait de Foie Gras, Les Epinards aux Croûtons, Jambon de Bayonne, Haricots Verts, Filet de Boeuf, Chapon du Mans, Bombe Glacée, Gelée d'Oranges, Petits Savarins au Kirsch, Meringues à la Chantilly, Bûche de Noël, Potage à la Tortue, Consommé Claire, Crême de Riz à la PolonaiseTête de Veau en Tortue, Petite Marmite, Salade de Homard, Barquettes d'Ecrevisses, Saumon Mayonnaise, Truite Saumonée Froide, Cailles à la Bordeaux, Salmis de Gelinottes, Riz de Veau, Filets de Sole Mornay, Canetons de Rouen à l'Archiduc, Les Poulets Gras au Cresson, Langue de Boeuf Fumée, Suprême de Volaille aux Truffes, Turbot Sauce Hollandaise, Oeufs de Pluviers, Parfait de Foie Gras, Les Epinards aux Croûtons, Jambon de Bayonne, Haricots Verts, Filet de Boeuf, Chapon du Mans, Bombe Glacée, Gelée d'Oranges, Petits Savarins au Kirsch, Meringues à la Chantilly, Bûche de Noël, Potage à la Tortue, Consommé Claire, Crême de Riz à la PolonaiseTête de Veau en Tortue, Petite Marmite, Salade de Homard, Barquettes d'Ecrevisses, Saumon Mayonnaise, Truite Saumonée Froide, Cailles à la Bordeaux, Salmis de Gelinottes, Riz de Veau, Filets de Sole Mornay, Canetons de Rouen à l'Archiduc, Les Poulets Gras au Cresson, Langue de Boeuf Fumée, Suprême de Volaille aux Truffes, Turbot Sauce Hollandaise, Oeufs de Pluviers, Parfait de Foie Gras, Les Epinards aux Croûtons, Jambon de Bayonne, Haricots Verts, Filet de Boeuf, Chapon du Mans, Bombe Glacée, Gelée d'Oranges, Petits Savarins au Kirsch, Meringues à la Chantilly, Bûche de Noël, Potage à la Tortue, Consommé Claire, Crême de Riz

State Banquets

There is a long tradition of kings, queens and presidents paying goodwill

visits abroad to cement alliances and renew friendships. These visits often

had a special importance both diplomatically and commercially, and were

particularly important in the years leading to World War I, as shown by the

visits illustrated of Emperor Wilhelm of Germany and President Poincaré of

France. In Britain, Queen Elizabeth II normally hosts two state visits per year.

A return banquet President Putin hosted for the Queen at Spencer House

in London before returning to Russia is illustrated. The USA also hosts

state visits with banquets, one of which is illustrated, the visit by the

President of Ireland in 1959 when they celebrated St Patrick's Day with

a grand dinner at the White House.

ENTERTAINMENT TO GENERAL GARIBALDI

ALL·WORSHIP·BE·TO·GOD·ONLY.

Fishmongers' Hall.

Thursday, April 21st, 1864.

PRIME WARDEN.

JAMES WESTON, Esq.

WARDENS.

JOSEPH UNDERWOOD, Esq.   FRAZER BRADSHAW HENSHAW, Esq.

JAMES SPICER, Esq.   GEORGE MOORE, Esq.

WALTER CHARLES VENNING, Esq.   W. B. TOWSE, Esq. CLERK.

PREMIER SERVICE.

Tortue à l'Anglaise.

Truites de Spey à l'Italienne.   Filets de Merlans à la Plessy.

Anguilles grillés à la Tartare.   Côtelettes de Saumon à l'Indienne.   Eperlans frits.

Saumon de Glaster bouille.   Turbot au Sauce d'Homard.

SECONDE SERVICE.

Cracouskys à la Polonaise.   Olives d'Huitres en fritures.

Filets de Cercelles au vin d'Oporto.   Ris d'Agneau au Petits Caisses.

Côtelettes d'Agneau aux Concombres.

Chapons farcis aux Truffes.   Petits Poulets aux Pois d'Asperge.

Jambons Sautés au vin de Madère.   Langues de Bœuf aux Epinards.   Pâtés à la Maitre d'Hotel.

Petits Poulet du Printemps rotis.

Quartiers d'Agneau rotis.   Selles de Mouton rotis.

TROISIEME SERVICE.

Canetons.   Dindonneaux piqués.   Oisons.

Mayonaisse d'Homard.   Crevettes en Bouquets.   Œufs de Pluviers en Buissons.

Tourtes à la Crème.   Geleés au Marasquin.   Crèmes aux Ananas.

Poudins Moelleux.   Croques en Bouche à l'Orange.   Gateau glacé aux Amandes.

Suedoises aux Millefruits.   Patisserie à la Florentine.   Feuilletage à l'Espagnol

Poudins de Savoie aux Conserves.   Meringue de Pommes à la Seville.

Poudins de Nesselrode.   Caviare à la Russe.

RING & BRYMER, 15, Cornhill.   Successors to BIRCH, BIRCH, & Co.

THE GREAT ITALIAN NATIONALIST
GENERAL GARIBALDI

A banquet was held in honour of General Garibaldi on his visit to London in 1864. The paper lace menu shown here is a wonderful souvenir of this occasion.

General Garibaldi had a tumultuous welcome in London with thousands of people lining the streets to see him arrive. While there he was presented with the Freedom of the City, a token of his services in the cause of liberty. He was a guest of the Duke of Sutherland, and was received by all except Queen Victoria, who violently disapproved. Even the Prince of Wales attended a reception.

Garibaldi was regarded as the hero of liberal nationalism, having devoted his life to the unification of Italy. From 1834, when he took part in a failed uprising in Piedmont, he worked tirelessly for the cause of unity. Exiled to Uruguay, he formed an Italian Legion in 1843 where they first wore the famous red shirts. In 1860 he landed in Sicily with 'The Thousand' and finally achieved the overthrow of the Kingdom of Naples, proclaiming himself ruler in the name of Victor Emmanuel II.

The menu for the banquet at Fishmongers' Hall is quite staggering, even by the standards of the day. There were 40 dishes, including seven fish dishes. Smelts are tiny sea and freshwater fish with a delicate flavour. There were 13 desserts to choose from, including Nesselrode pudding, a rich combination of custard cream, chestnut purée, crystallized and dried fruits and whipped cream, frozen in a mould and turned out, and the spectacular croquembouche, a towering mound of sugar-glazed orange segments on a pastry base, decorated with spun sugar and glazed glacé cherries.

Left: The delicate paper lace menu for the banquet given for General Garibaldi in 1864.

The Italian Nationalist General Garibaldi.

MENU
Turtle Soup
Spey Trout with Mushrooms
Fillets of Whiting
Grilled Eel with Tartare Sauce
Salmon Steaks with Curry Sauce
Fried Smelts
Boiled Salmon
Turbot with Lobster Sauce

Chicken Croquettes
Fried Oysters
Fillets of Wild Duck in Port
Sweetbread Tartlets
Lamb Chops with Cucumber
Capons Stuffed with Truffles
Baby Chickens with Asparagus Peas
Ham Braised in Madeira
Tongue with Spinach
Pies with Savoury Butter
Roast Spring Chicken
Roast Quarters of Lamb
Roast Saddle of Lamb

Ducks
Spiced Young Turkeys
Goslings
Lobster Mayonnaise
Prawns
Plovers' Eggs

Cream Tarts
Ices with Maraschino
Pineapple Creams
Creamy Puddings
Orange Croquembouche
Iced Cake with Almonds
Moulded Fruit Jellies
Florentine Pastries
Spanish Pastries
Savoie Puddings with Conserves
Apple Meringues
Nesselrode Pudding
Caviar

❦1873❦
IN HONOUR OF THE SHAH
Nasir al-Din, Shah of Persia

Nasir al-Din ruled Persia, now Iran, for the second half of the 19th century (1848–96). In 1873 the Shah set out on a grand world-wide voyage that was to take him to Russia, Germany, Belgium, England, France, Switzerland, Italy, Austria, Turkey and Georgia.

This menu was for the banquet given in his honour by the Lord Mayor and Corporation of the City of London on 20 June at the Guildhall. The elaborate design of the menu, beautifully illustrated and gilded, refers to Persian art and architectural style and recreates the intricate patterning found in the palaces of the period.

The Shah made three trips to Europe – in 1873, 1878 and 1889. He was a reforming ruler, and was responsible for modernizing Persia. He built roads, opened European-style schools and collected European art.

Persia at the time was very much a pawn in the 'Great Game' between Britain and Russia, being a buffer state between these two nations. The economy was in effect controlled by British monopolies and concessions, such as the railway and the telegraph.

On this visit in 1873 Prime Minister Gladstone persuaded Queen Victoria to entertain the Shah, whom she described as her 'oriental brother'. Fortunately, she found him suitably polite and dignified, and in his honour she wore the Koh-i-noor diamond, the Indian diamond that the British acquired from an Indian Maharajah.

Queen Victoria was not present at the banquet at the Guildhall, which was obviously a predominantly business occasion. History does not record what the Shah of Persia made of the menu, which included such solidly English items as wild boar's head, pickled ox tongue and pigeon pie. 'Palestine' creams were probably so-called for his benefit, and may have been specially flavoured or spiced. We do not know what 'Ponche' jelly was.

MENU
Salmon Mayonnaise
Lobsters

Boned, Stuffed Chicken, Garnished
with Truffles
Hors d'Oeuvres in Aspic
Game Paté in Aspic
Pigeon Pie

Wild Boar's Head

Roast Chicken
Ham in Aspic
Pickled Ox Tongue

Boiled Chicken
Chicken Garnished with Asparagus
Tips and Truffles

Pressed Beef
Roast Beef
Roast Lamb
Lobster Salad

Fruit Jelly
Ponche Jelly
Wine Jelly
Palestine Creams
French Pastries Poached fruit

ENTERTAINMENT
TO HIS MAJESTY
THE SHAH OF PERSIA
AT THE
GUILDHALL,
Friday 20th June 1873

BY THE
RIGHT HON. THE LORD MAYOR
AND THE
CORPORATION OF THE
CITY OF LONDON.

MENU

MAYONNAISE DE SAUMON.

BUISSONS DE HOMARD.

GALANTINE DE VOLAILLE À LA PÉRIGORD.

ASPICS DE SALPICON.

PÂTÉS DE GIBIER EN ASPIC.

PÂTE DE PIGEON À L'ESSENCE.

HURES DE SANGLIER.

POULETS RÔTIS.   JAMBONS EN ASPIC.

LANGUES DE BŒUF À L'ECARLATE.

POULETS BOUILLIS.   POULETS À LA PRINCESSE.

PRESSED BEEF.   ROAST BEEF.

QUARTIERS D'AGNEAU RÔTIS.

SALAD DE HOMARD.

GELÉE À LA MACEDOINE.   GELÉE DE PONCHE.

GELÉE AU VIN À LA MODERNE.

CRÊMES À LA PALESTINE.

PATISSERIE À LA PARISIENNE.

COMPOTES DE FRUITS.

The ALBION,   Aldersgate Street.

THE RIGHT HONOURABLE SIR SYDNEY H. WATERLOW, KNT. LORD MAYOR

Sheriffs. { THOMAS WHITE ESQ. ALDERMAN | Under Sheriffs { ARTHUR TURNER HEWITT ESQ
FREDERICK PERKINS. ESQ | ALEXANDER CROSLEY. ESQ

M. MC GEORGE. ESQ. CHAIRMAN

Corporation of London.
Reception of Their Imperial Majesties
The German Emperor and Empress
Wednesday 13th November, 1907.

Domine — dirige — nos.

The menu cover for the banquet given at the Guildhall for Emperor Wilhelm II in 1907. It shows the Imperial eagle, together with vignettes of the Guildhall (top left and right) and Windsor Castle (bottom).

A GOODWILL VISIT

EMPEROR WILHELM II OF GERMANY

The he German Emperor Wilhelm II came to England in November 1907 on a goodwill visit. In his speech at the Guildhall after this dinner on 13 November he attempted to allay fears that the build-up of his navy was directed at hostilities against England.

Relations between Britain and Germany had become more and more strained, each being suspicious of the other in this period known as the 'Armaments Race' in the run-up to World War I – this in spite of the fact that King Edward VII was actually Wilhelm's uncle. Britain had already formed the Entente Cordiale with the French, and in 1907 this became the Triple Entente with the addition of Russia to the alliance.

During the visit Wilhelm was invited on board the royal yacht. He instructed his chancellor to approach Edward and suggest forming an alliance between the two countries. But Edward is reported to have said that the alliance was 'not worthwhile . . . in view of the absence of any cause for discord or ill-will'.

The Emperor Wilhelm II of Germany

MENU
Turtle Soup
Clear Turtle Soup

A Round of Soles
Lobster in Cream Sauce

Casserole of Partridges with
Wine and Mushrooms

Lamb Chops Garnished
with Mushrooms and
Truffles
Pheasants with Foie Gras

Barons of Beef

Baby Chickens Stuffed with
Chestnuts
Braised Tongue
Game Pies

Moulded Fruit Jelly
Custard Creams Flavoured
with Liqueur
Tangerine Jelly
Clear Jelly
Pastries with Golden Plums
Mixed Fruit

Ice Creams
Dessert

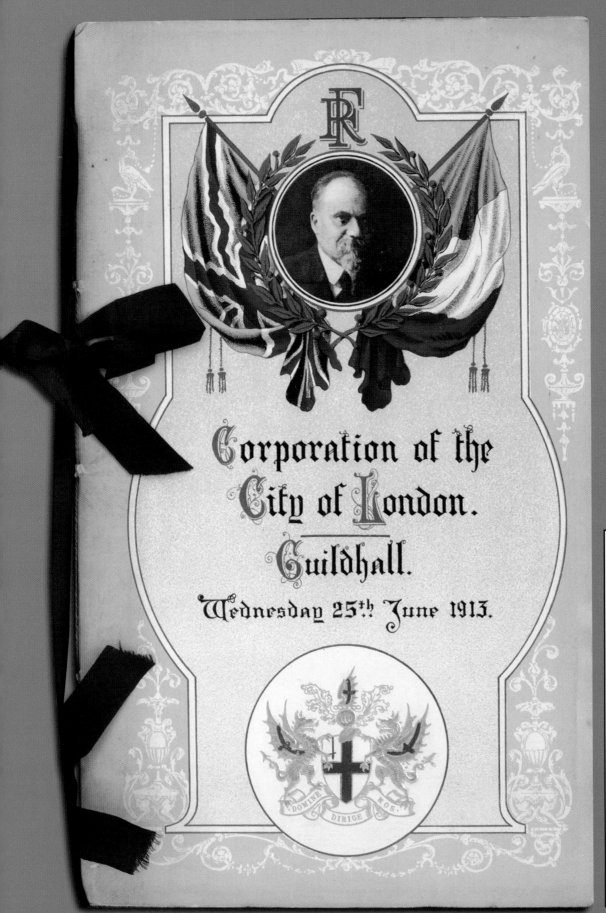

The menu for the banquet at the Guildhall in honour of President Poincaré shows both the British and French flags.

E R

Corporation of the City of London.

Guildhall.

Wednesday 25th June 1913.

DOMINE DIRIGE NOS

MENU
Turtle Soup
Clear Turtle Soup

Salmon Mayonnaise
Lobster Salad

Quail in Wine Sauce

Lamb Chops with Tomatoes

Baron of Beef

Chicken in White Sauce

Smoked Tongue

Orange Jelly
French Meringues
Pineapple Cream
Bavarian Fruit Cream
Maids of Honour
French Pastries

Ices
Dessert

ON THE BRINK OF WAR IN EUROPE
PRESIDENT POINCARÉ OF FRANCE

In June 1913 a banquet was held at the Guildhall in the City of London on the occasion of the state visit of the new President of the French Republic, Raymond Poincaré. Britain and France had become close allies following the signing of the Entente Cordiale in 1904, a fact underlined by this visit.

Poincaré was both a conservative and a nationalist and so he proceeded to strengthen France to face possible hostilities. A bill increasing military service to three years was passed, and the French alliances with Great Britain and Russia were tightened. This visit helped to strengthen these alliances.

The end of the Balkan wars coincided with a time of increasing tension between the major powers, with the Triple Entente (France-Britain-Russia) on one side, and the Central Powers (Germany and the Austro-Hungarian Empire) on the other. Only a year after this visit World War I began.

As usual, this is a menu designed to impress. The most spectacular item is the baron of beef, or double sirloin, for serious meat eaters. The Bavarian fruit cream is also impressive, and very rich. It is set in an elaborate mould, chilled, then turned out. Maids of honour are little pastry cakes, filled with curd cheese, egg, almonds, sugar, currants and brandy.

THE CRYPT.
Under Guildhall.—(XV. Century).

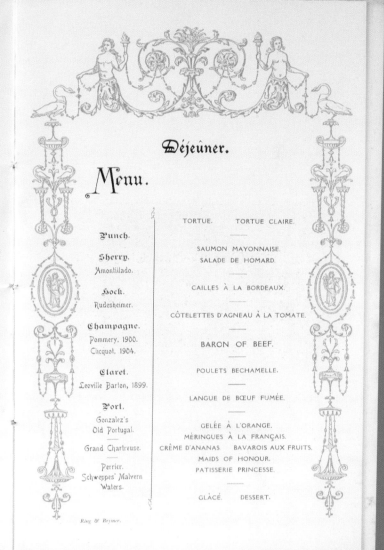

Déjeûner.

Menu.

Punch.

Sherry.
Amontillado.

Hock.
Rudesheimer.

Champagne.
Pommery, 1900.
Clicquot, 1904.

Claret.
Leoville Barton, 1899.

Port.
Gonzalez's
Old Portugal.

Grand Chartreuse.

Perrier.
Schweppes' Malvern
Waters.

TORTUE.   TORTUE CLAIRE.

SAUMON MAYONNAISE.
SALADE DE HOMARD.

CAILLES À LA BORDEAUX.

CÔTELETTES D'AGNEAU À LA TOMATE.

BARON OF BEEF.

POULETS BECHAMELLE.

LANGUE DE BŒUF FUMÉE.

GELÉE À L'ORANGE.
MÉRINGUES À LA FRANÇAIS.
CRÊME D'ANANAS   BAVAROIS AUX FRUITS.
MAIDS OF HONOUR.
PATISSERIE PRINCESSE.

GLACÉ.   DESSERT.

Ring & Brymer.

COLD WAR INTRIGUE
BULGANIN AND KHRUSHCHEV OF THE USSR

In April 1956, during the Cold War period, President Bulganin of the USSR and Nikita Khrushchev, Head of the Communist Party, made a goodwill visit to Britain, a visit which almost turned into a diplomatic disaster. In 1955 a naval frogman, Lionel Crabb (known as Buster Crabb), had been asked to dive and inspect the hull of the Soviet cruiser *Sverdlov*, in British waters to take part in the Spithead Naval Review. Crabb and another diver, Sydney Knowles, dived under the *Sverdlov* by night and found at the bow of the ship a large circular opening in the bottom of the hull. Crabb went up inside the hole and examined a large propeller, which appeared to be able to be lowered and directed to give thrust to the bow.

As the mission was a success, it was decided to ask Crabb to look at the hull of the cruiser *Orzhonikidze*, which was bringing Krushchev and Bulganin to Britain, this time to search for special anti-sonar gear and mine-laying hatches. Crabb was never seen alive again. The *Orzhonikidze* left and a story broke in Fleet Street that the famous wartime frogman, Buster Crabb, had failed to surface following a dive near Portsmouth. The Admiralty stated that Commander Crabb was missing, presumed drowned, following a dive with secret equipment 3 miles (4km) from Portsmouth harbour where the Russian ship had been berthed. This fuelled a mystery that was to last for years.

On inspection, reporters found that the register pages at the hotel where Crabb was staying were torn out, showing no mention of Crabb or his colleagues. The Soviet Ambassador protested to the Foreign Office regarding a frogman being sited near the Russian ships in Portsmouth, demanding an explanation. Questions were asked in the House of Commons, but the Government refused to comment.

Some time later Crabb's body was found, headless and handless, identified by his old-fashioned Navy frogman suit. On his headstone it reads, 'In Loving Memory of my son, Commander Lionel Crabb RNVR GM OBE At rest at last.'

The menu for this lunch at the Guildhall consists of solid British fare, no doubt much appreciated by the two Russians. Krushchev came from peasant stock and was noted for his fondness for endless toasts in vodka.

Nikita Krushchev, Head of the Communist Party in the USSR.

THE MISSING FROGMAN

The case of the missing frogman baffled everyone at the time. Royal Navy Commander Lionel Crabb was reported missing and presumed dead in April 1956 after he disappeared on a mysterious diving operation in Portsmouth harbour. Crabb vanished while the Russian cruiser *Orzhonikidze* and two Soviet destroyers were berthed in Portsmouth harbour. The *Orzhonikidze* had brought Soviet leaders President Nikolai Bulganin and Communist party boss Nikita Khrushchev to Britain for an official visit.

It was noted by the Press that no apparent search of the harbour had been made since, indicating that the Admiralty had some knowledge of Crabb's whereabouts, dead or alive. His hotel room had been cleared of his belongings and the relevant pages in the hotel register had been torn out. The body was subsequently found, headless and handless, near Chichester.

Lionel (Buster) Crabb, Royal Navy Commander, wearing part of his frogman's outfit.

Wines

Menu

CLEAR TURTLE

PUNCH,
Birch's

FILLETS OF DOVER SOLE

Burton brewed
PALE ALE

or

CHAMPAGNE,
Louis Roederer,
Cristal Brut 1949

ROAST SCOTCH BEEF
Horseradish Sauce
New Jersey Potatoes and
Garden Peas

COMMONWEALTH ALE
Brewed 1953

BAKED APPLE DUMPLINGS
Devonshire Cream

LIQUEUR WHISKY,
Macallan Glenlivet
15 years old

or

BRANDY,
Bisquit Dubouche
1937

STILTON and
CAERPHILLY
Cheeses

Coffee

Toasts

THE QUEEN

THE CHAIRMAN
OF THE PRÆSIDIUM OF THE
SUPREME SOVIET OF THE U.S.S.R.

OUR SOVIET GUESTS

THE LORD MAYOR
AND CORPORATION OF LONDON

Programme of Music

1. March	..	NEW CENTURY	..	Henry Steel
2. Overture	..	THE ARCADIANS		Monckton and Talbot
3. Rapsodie	..	RUSSE	..	Elric Olsen
4. Selection from		SWAN LAKE		Tchaikovsky
5. Melodies from		WHITE HORSE INN		Benatzky and Stolz
6. Waltz	..	THE CUCKOO	..	J. Lally
7. Selection	..	SALAD DAYS		Julian Slade
8. Suite	..	THREE DALE DANCES		.. A. Wood
9. Waltz Fantasia		TCHAIKOVSKY		Arr. Don Bowden
10. Finale	..	IN TOWN TONIGHT		Eric Coates

by the
STRING ORCHESTRA OF THE HONOURABLE ARTILLERY COMPANY
under the direction of
W. A. CRIGHTON, Band Master
by permission of the Commanding Officer

CORPORATION OF LONDON

LUNCHEON

to Mr. BULGANIN
Chairman of the Council of Ministers of the U.S.S.R. and

Mr. KHRUSCHEV
Member of the Praesidium of the Supreme Soviet of the U.S.S.R.

MANSION HOUSE
20th April 1956

ST PATRICK'S DAY AT THE WHITE HOUSE

DINNER GIVEN BY PRESIDENT EISENHOWER FOR PRESIDENT O'KELLY OF IRELAND

This is a menu to celebrate the state visit of President Sean O'Kelly of Ireland to the US in 1959 and the St Patrick's Day dinner at the White House on 17 March.

Sean O'Kelly was involved in the Easter Rising in Ireland, 1916, the most famous attempt by militant republicans to seize control of Ireland and force independence from the United Kingdom. The event is seen as a key point on the road to Irish independence. After joining Sinn Féin in 1916, O'Kelly was elected Sinn Féin MP in 1918. Along with other Sinn Féin MPs, he refused to take his seat in Westminster. Instead they set up an illegal Irish parliament, called Dáil Éireann, in Dublin. O'Kelly served as Speaker or Ceann Comhairle of Dáil Éireann. He also served as the Irish Republic's official but unaccepted Ambassador, who sought and was refused admittance to the post-World War I peace treaty negotiations at Versailles in France.

Sean O'Kelly was elected President of Ireland in 1945 by a popular vote of the people, defeating two other candidates, and he was re-elected unopposed to the presidency a second time in 1952. He retired at the end of his second term in 1959 and died in 1966, 50 years after the Easter Rising that first brought him to prominence.

On his retirement as President in 1959 he was described as a 'model president' by the normally hostile *Irish Times*. Though controversial, he was widely loved as a funny, honourable, occasionally flawed but always decent man.

It was a hearty dinner. Seafood Newburg (usually lobster) is served in a rich cream and sherry sauce. Eggplant is the American word for aubergine. The beans 'almondine' were probably tossed with toasted almonds in butter.

Below left: President Eisenhower at his desk.

Below right: The White House.

DINNER

Prosciutto Ham and Melon

Cream of Water Cress Soup

Dry Sack   Melba Toast

Celery Hearts   Assorted Olives

Chateau   Seafood Newburg
Climens   Vol-au-Vent
1950   Cucumber Sandwiches

Beaune   Roast Stuffed Long Island Duckling
Greves   Applesauce
1952   Casserole of Eggplant
French String Beans Almondine

Tossed Greens in Salad with Anchovy
Cheese Crusts

Pol Roger
1952

Frosted Mint Delight
Lady Fingers

Assorted Nuts   Bon Bons   Demitasse
Mints

THE WHITE HOUSE
Tuesday, March 17, 1959

THE OPENING OF THE ST LAWRENCE SEAWAY

QUEEN ELIZABETH II AND PRESIDENT EISENHOWER

H.M.Y. BRITANNIA

OPENING OF THE ST. LAWRENCE SEAWAY
26th JUNE, 1959

Oeufs Mollets Lucullus

Demi Poussin Poële St. Lambert
Choufleur Mornay
Pommes Nouvelles Rissolées
Salade Romaine

Bombe Glacée aux Fraises
Macédoine de Fruits
Gaufrettes

The St Lawrence Seaway is one of the world's most comprehensive inland navigation systems, linking the Great Lakes to the Atlantic Ocean. It was officially opened in 1959 by Queen Elizabeth II, representing Canada, and President Eisenhower, and to mark the occasion a lunch was held on board the Royal Yacht *Britannia*. Present at the lunch were the Queen and Prince Philip, President and Mrs Eisenhower and President Diefenbaker of Canada and Mrs Diefenbaker.

Initial construction work had begun in 1954, involving cooperation between the Canadian and American governments. Overall, the project cost 470 million US dollars, of which $336.2 million were paid by Canada and $133.8 million by the United States. Income from the operating of the Seaway is shared accordingly.

The St Lawrence Seaway was opened on 25 April 1959 and the official opening ceremonies were held two months later on 26 June in the presence of Queen Elizabeth II and President Dwight D. Eisenhower.

Crowds cheered, sirens wailed and bands played as the Royal Yacht *Britannia* began the first leg of the 2,300 mile journey from Montreal to the Atlantic. The Queen left the yacht for the airfield to meet President Eisenhower. *Britannia* cruised up the Seaway to Valleyfield, landing the President and other guests at Lower Beauharnois Lock, and on reaching the opening ceremony site the cars carrying the Queen and the President arrived. A royal salute was fired by the support ship *Gatineau*, together with the USS *Forrest Sherman* and HMS *Ulster*. These three ships formed the international escort. On reaching St Lambert waving crowds assembled to greet the royal party and heads of state. On Lake St Louis 16 Canadian and US warships assembled, the

sailors cheering the Queen and the President as they passed. At five o'clock in the afternoon *Britannia* entered Lower Beauharnois Lock and the President and his party disembarked. One of the escort ships fired a salute, ending a long and memorable day.

The Royal Yacht Britannia, *with President Eisenhower and Queen Elizabeth II aboard, passes through the St Lambert Lock at the opening of the St Lawrence Seaway on 26 June 1959. Two Canadian Coast Guard vessels led the ship through the lock at the Montreal entry.*

MENU

Soft-Boiled Eggs in White Sauce on
Artichoke Hearts, Garnished with
Sweetbreads, Truffles and Mushrooms

Half Baby Chicken, Braised
Cauliflower in Cheese Sauce
Sautéed New Potatoes
Salad

Strawberry Ice Cream Mould
Fruit Salad
Waffles

STATE BANQUET

IN HONOUR OF

THE PRESIDENT

OF THE

FRENCH REPUBLIC

AND

MADAME JACQUES CHIRAC

BUCKINGHAM PALACE

TUESDAY, 14th MAY, 1996

Above: President Chirac travels with Queen Elizabeth in a carriage procession down the Mall to Buckingham Palace, May 1996.

Le Menu

Consommé Célestine

———

Roulade de Sole à la Mousse de Homard
Sauce Safran et Ciboulettes

———

Carré d'Agneau aux Légumes de Printemps
Asperges au Beurre
Pommes Cretan
Salade

———

Pêches Toscane

Les Vins

Chassagne Montrachet, Morgeot 1988
Château Pichon Longueville,
Comtesse de Lalande 1982
Louis Roederer 1986
Warre 1970

Music Programme

March	CEREMONIAL PROCESSION	
Waltz	WESTMINSTER WALTZ	
Selection	BEST OF THE BEATLES	
Vive La France	FRENCH FESTIVAL	
String Feature	AIN'T MISBEHAVIN	
Selection	BROADWAY TONIGHT	
Song	SOMEWHERE OUT THERE	
Polka	TRITSCH-TRATSCH	
Selection	SOUVENIRS DE FRANCE	
Waltz	BY THE SLEEPY LAGOON	
Selection	ANDREW LLOYD WEBBER	
Piano Feature	FORGOTTEN DREAMS	
Show Feature	LES MISERABLES	
March	ARMS PARK	

Major S. A. WAT...
Director of Music, Welsh Gua...

Pipe Programme

March	STAR OF THE COUNTY DOWN
Strathspey	STRUAN ROBERTSON
Reel	COLONEL MACLEOD
March	ST. PATRICK'S DAY

Pipe Major R. TUMELTY
1st Battalion, Irish Guards

FRENCH CUISINE AT BUCKINGHAM PALACE

BANQUET GIVEN BY QUEEN ELIZABETH II FOR PRESIDENT CHIRAC OF FRANCE

A state banquet was held at Buckingham Palace in May 1996 in honour of the new President of the French Republic, Jacques Chirac, who had been elected in 1995.

The top table included several members of the royal family, including the Duke of Edinburgh, the Prince of Wales, Princess Anne, Prince Edward and Princess Margaret. Seated between the royal princes was Madame Simone Veil, first president of the European Parliament and who, as a young woman, was in a Nazi concentration camp.

President Chirac blew kisses to the crowd as he travelled down the Mall with the Queen in an open carriage, en route for Buckingham Palace. Later he met British party leaders at the Palace to talk about a variety of topics, including the uproar over BSE or 'mad cow disease', and the subsequent European Union ban on British beef. He was reported as saying that Paris would support a partial lifting of the ban.

At the start of his four-day visit President Chirac lunched at Buckingham Palace. On the menu that day was fillet of beef, which the President duly ate. But at the state banquet, a more public occasion, lamb was tactfully on the menu, not beef. In his speech after dinner President Chirac appealed to Britain to work more closely with France on building up Europe.

The menu is in striking contrast to state banquets of the past, with their six or seven courses and numerous heavy dishes. This is a light, elegant menu, and suitably French. The clear soup has a special garnish: small pancakes are stuffed with a mixture of diced chicken, egg and brandy, then thinly sliced. Each soup plate has two tablespoons of these slices as garnish. Cretan Potatoes must be a special invention of the Buckingham Palace chefs.

MENU

Clear Soup, Garnished with Slices of Stuffed Pancake

Fillets of Sole Stuffed with Lobster, with Saffron and Chive Sauce

Loin of Lamb with Spring Vegetables
Asparagus with Butter Sauce
Cretan Potatoes
Salad

Peaches

The seating plan for the state banquet at Buckingham Palace in honour of President Chirac, 14 May 1996.

THE QUEEN

THE PRESIDENT OF THE FRENCH REPUBLIC	THE DUKE OF EDINBURGH
The Princess Royal	MADAME JACQUES CHIRAC
Monsieur Hervé de Charette	The Prince of Wales
The Princess Margaret, Countess of Snowdon	Madame le Ministre Simone Veil
The Archbishop of Canterbury	The Prince Edward

Left outer column:
The Duchess of Gloucester · The Lord Chancellor · Mrs Major · The Duke of Kent · Princess Michael of Kent · The Prime Minister · The Ambassador of the French Republic · The Countess of Airlie · The Viscount Slim · Madame Catherine Colonna · The Secretary of State for Health · Dame Jennifer Jenkins · Monsieur Philippe de Bourgoing · The Lady Susan Hussey · The Lord Sterling of Plaistow · The Lady Mayoress · The Ambassador of Italy · Lady Mallaby · Monsieur de Larosière de Champfeu · The Rt Hon Paddy Ashdown MP · Lady Nicholson · Sir Robin Butler · Mrs Wickremesinghe · Sir Ewen Fergusson · Madame de Larosière de Champfeu · Sir Geoffrey de Bellaigue · Mrs Barrington · Lieutenant General Sir Rupert Smith · Sir Bryan Nicholson · Madame Taix · Mr Michael Jay · Mr Howard Davies · Lady Morton · Mr Richard Branson · Mrs Trimble · Major General Iain Mackay-Dick · The Hon Lady Weatherall · Mr David Peppercorn · Mrs Figgis · Mr Phillip Young · Mrs Andrew

Inner table, left side:
The Lord Richard · Viscountess Cranborne · The Apostolic Nuncio · The Duchess of Norfolk · The Lord Weinstock · Monsieur Gilbert Gantier · The Lady Bramall · The High Commissioner for Canada · The Baroness Hogg · Field Marshal the Lord Bramall · Mrs Attoungbré · The Minister of Agriculture, Fisheries and Food · Monsieur Philippe Coste · The Lady Jane Fellowes · The Rt Hon the Lord Mayor of London · Lady Inge · The High Commissioner for Sri Lanka · Lady Greenbury · The Lord Chesham · Signora Galli · Mr David Trimble MP · Lady Smith · Major Sir Shane Blewitt · Colonel Peer de Jong · Lady Hanson · Brigadier Miles Hunt-Davis · Professor Barbara Young · Monsieur Patrick Ponsolle · Mr Alistair Horne · Mrs Serena Sutcliffe · Monsieur Jean-Paul Taix · Mrs Peat · Mr Rob Andrew · Madame Rambosson · Mr Robin Janvrin · Mrs Davies · Mr Hugh Roberts · Mrs Branson

Inner table, right side:
The Lord Camoys · The Viscountess Slim · The Ambassador of the Republic of Côte d'Ivoire · The Lady Richard · The Lord Privy Seal · Mrs Rayananonda · Secretary of State for Foreign and Commonwealth Affairs · Monsieur Jean-David Levitte · The Lady Sterling of Plaistow · The Ambassador of Thailand · The Lord Jenkins of Hillhead · Mrs Rifkind · Monsieur Pierre Menat · The Rt Hon Sir Robert Fellowes · Mrs Dorrell · Field Marshal Sir Peter Inge · The Ambassador of the Federal Republic of Germany · Lady Fergusson · Monsieur Jean-Claude Trichet · Mrs Ashdown · Sir Alastair Morton · Mr Richard Lambert · Lady Graydon · Sir John Coles · Monsieur Jacques Rambosson · Lady de Bellaigue · Sir John Hanson · Mrs Horne · Mr John Monks · The Lady Glenconner · Mr John Galliano · Monsieur Michel Bourdin · Mrs Ayling · Mr Michael Peat · Madame Bourdin · Mr Anthony Figgis · Lieutenant Colonel Seymour Gilbert-Denham · Mrs Gibson

Right outer column:
The Lady Mackay of Clashfern · Monsieur Dominique de Villepin · Princess Alexandra, The Hon Lady Ogilvy · The Duke of Gloucester · Mrs Carey · Prince Michael of Kent · The Duchess of Grafton · The Hon Sir Angus Ogilvy · The Rt Hon The Speaker · The Earl Marshal · The Lady Camoys · Vice-Amiral d'Escadre Delaunay · The Lady Weinstock · The Earl of Airlie · Monsieur Daniel Jouanneau · Lady Butler · The High Commissioner for The Republic of South Africa · The Lady Chesham · The Lord Chief Justice · Dr Tshabalala-Msimang · Sir Christopher Mallaby · Madame Ponsolle · The Ambassador of the Republic of Ireland · Mr Robin Cook MP · Lady Coles · Sir Richard Greenbury · Mrs Oesterhelt · Air Chief Marshal Sir Michael Graydon · Lady Dugdale · Monsieur Christopher Thiery · Mrs Jay · Monsieur Veil · Mrs Janvrin · Professor Robert Gibson · Mr George Simpson · Mrs Monks · Vice Admiral Sir James Weatherall · Mrs Simpson · Lieutenant Colonel Malcolm Ross · Mr Robert Ayling · Mrs Mackay-Dick

Bottom: Major General Sir Simon Cooper — The Viscount Ridley

AFTER THE THAW

DINNER GIVEN FOR QUEEN ELIZABETH II BY PRESIDENT PUTIN OF RUSSIA

At the end of his state visit to Britain in 2003 the Russian leader Vladimir Putin gave a banquet for the Queen at Spencer House. There had been a state banquet held at Buckingham Palace in honour of Mr and Mrs Putin on the first day of their visit, 24 June, and it is customary for the visiting head of state to host a return dinner for the Sovereign before leaving the country. President Putin was the first Russian leader to make an official state visit to Britain for more than a century. The last Russian leader to make a state visit to Britain was Tsar Alexander II in 1874.

During his stay the Russian leader visited Edinburgh, celebrating the strong connections between Russia and Scotland. He paid tribute to the work of Scottish architects Charles Cameron and William Hastie who built many of the bridges and buildings in St Petersburg. Mr Putin also held talks with Tony Blair and held a press conference at the Foreign and Commonwealth Office. The return banquet for the Queen and the Duke of Edinburgh was held at Spencer House in London on 26 June 2003.

The menu, in both Russian and English, is very attractive and decorated with a view of old St Petersburg. The dinner began with the Russian delicacy Rasstegai pie – pastry boats made with a yeast dough and filled with pike stuffing.

Attractively laid table for guests at the banquet given by President Putin for the Queen and Duke of Edinburgh at Spencer House.

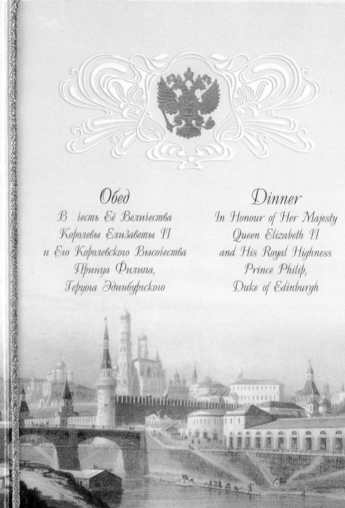

Обед

В честь Её Величества
Королевы Елизаветы II
и Его Королевского Высочества
Принца Филипа,
Герцога Эдинбургского

Dinner

In Honour of Her Majesty
Queen Elizabeth II
and His Royal Highness
Prince Philip,
Duke of Edinburgh

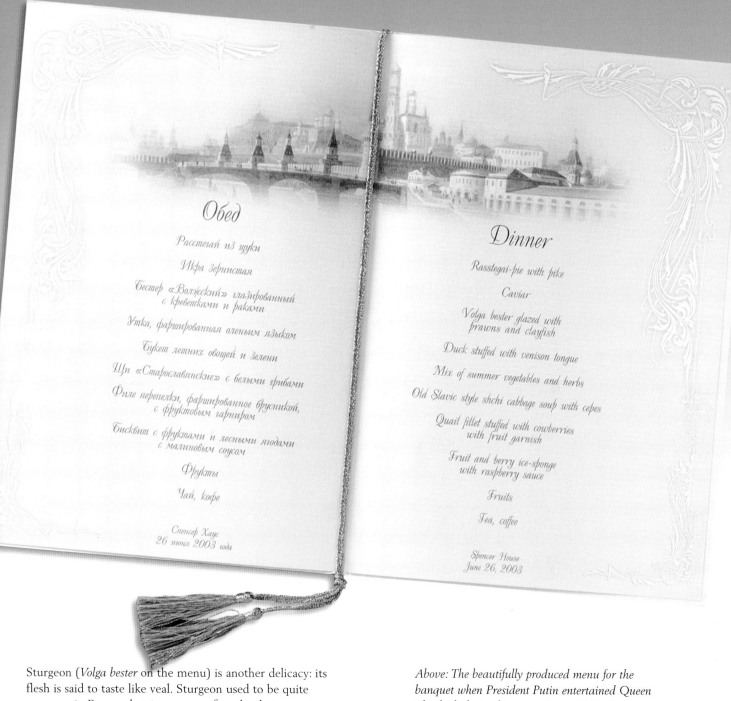

Обед

Расстегай из щуки

Икра зернистая

Бестер «Волжский» глазированный
с креветками и раками

Утка, фаршированная оленьим языком

Букет летних овощей и зелени

Щи «Старославянские» с белыми грибами

Филе перепелки, фаршированное брусникой,
с фруктовым гарниром

Бисквит с фруктами и лесными ягодами
с малиновым соусом

Фрукты

Чай, кофе

Спенсер Хаус
26 июня 2003 года

Dinner

Rasstegai-pie with pike

Caviar

Volga bester glazed with
prawns and clayfish

Duck stuffed with venison tongue

Mix of summer vegetables and herbs

Old Slavic style shchi cabbage soup with cepes

Quail fillet stuffed with cowberries
with fruit garnish

Fruit and berry ice-sponge
with raspberry sauce

Fruits

Tea, coffee

Spencer House
June 26, 2003

Sturgeon (*Volga bester* on the menu) is another delicacy: its flesh is said to taste like veal. Sturgeon used to be quite common in Europe, but is now rare, found only in certain rivers in France, Spain and Russia, though it still thrives in the US. Cowberries, used to stuff the quail fillet, are better known as bilberries.

Above: The beautifully produced menu for the banquet when President Putin entertained Queen Elizabeth during his state visit in 2003. It shows a view of Old St Petersburg.

onnaise, Truite Saumonée Froide, Cailles à la Bordeaux , Salmis de Ge...

...lets Gras au Cresson, Langue de Boeuf Fumée, Suprême de Volaille aux...

...ards aux Croûtons, Jambon de Bayonne, Haricots Verts, Filet de Boeu...

...ingues à la Chantilly, Bûche de Noël, Potage à la Tortue, Consommé C...

...omard, Barquettes d'Ecrevisses, Saumon Mayonnaise, Truite Saumoné...

...rnay, Canetons de Rouen à l'Archiduc, Les Poulets Gras au Cresson, La...

...ts de Pluviers, Parfait de Foie Gras, Les Epinards aux Croûtons, Jambo...

...e d'Oranges, Petits Savarins au Kirsch, Meringues à la Chantilly, Bûc...

...eau en Tortue, Petite Marmite, Salade de Homard, Barquettes d'Ecrevi...

...Gelinottes, Riz de Veau, Filets de Sole Mornay, Canetons de Rouen à l'...

...Truffes, Turbot Sauce Hollandaise, Oeufs de Pluviers, Parfait de Foie...

...uf, Chapon du Mans, Bombe Glacée, Gelée d'Oranges, Petits Savarins a...

...ue, Crême de Riz à la PolonaiseTête de Veau en Tortue, Petite Ma...

...monée Froide, Cailles à la Bordeaux , Salmis de Gelinottes, Riz de Vea...

...on, Langue de Boeuf Fumée, Suprême de Volaille aux Truffes, Turb...

...tons, Jambon de Bayonne, Haricots Verts, Filet de Boeuf, Chapon du...

...hantilly, Bûche de Noël, Potage à la Tortue, Consommé Claire, Crême d...

...quettes d'Ecrevisses, Saumon Mayonnaise, Truite Saumonée Froide, C...

...etons de Rouen à l'Archiduc, Les Poulets Gras au Cresson, Langue de B...

...iers, Parfait de Foie Gras, Les Epinards aux Croûtons, Jambon de B...

...ranges, Petits Savarins au Kirsch, Meringues à la Chantilly, Bûche de...

...u en Tortue, Petite Marmite, Salade de Homard, Barquettes d'Ecreviss...

...Gelinottes, Riz de Veau, Filets de Sole Mornay, Canetons de Rouen à l'...

...Truffes, Turbot Sauce Hollandaise, Oeufs de Pluviers, Parfait de Foie...

...uf, Chapon du Mans, Bombe Glacée, Gelée d'Oranges, Petits Savari...

...fes, Turbot Sauce Hollandaise, Oeufs de Pluviers, Parfait de Voie Gra...

...ron du Mans, Bombe Glacée, Gelée d'Oranges, Petits Savarins au Kir...

...e de Riz à la PolonaiseTête de Veau en Tortue, Petite Marmite,...

Dining at Sea

The great ocean liners hold a special place in the hearts of many, and the first half of the 20th century, up to the beginning of World War II, was their heyday. Passengers who were wealthy enough to travel in this way enjoyed unsurpassed luxury, with gala and carnival nights, dining and dancing in the wonderful surroundings of these floating palaces. Every evening there would be a seat at the captain's table for a few of the most important passengers, making the whole voyage a memorable experience. But not all was plain sailing. The sinking of the *Titanic* in 1912 sent a shiver through all would-be sea travellers, and later the Great Depression saw a significant fall in the number of passengers. But all that was forgotten by the time Cunard decided to build the *Queen Mary*. The launch of this beautiful liner was heralded as the greatest achievement in the history of British shipbuilding and marked a new era in ocean travel.

∽ 1911 ∾

MURDER, MAYHEM AND GOLD BULLION
The SS *Laurentic*

This dinner menu, for 27 June 1911, is from the liner SS *Laurentic*. The ship was built in 1905 by Harland and Wolff for the White Star Line, the same company that owned the *Titanic*. In 1910 this ship played an important part in apprehending the infamous murderer Dr Crippen, who was on board the Canadian Pacific SS *Montrose*, bound for Canada.

The *Montrose* was one of the very few liners fitted with a Marconi wireless radio, similar to that on the *Titanic*. The captain, Henry Kendall, recognized Crippen, in spite of the fact that he was in disguise and his mistress, Ethel Le Neve, was dressed as a young man. On 22 July he asked the radio operator to contact the Canadian Pacific offices in Liverpool, which he did via Poldhu in Cornwall. They in turn informed Scotland Yard. Kendall's information about the suspects had taken five hours to reach Inspector Dew, who was in charge of the case, but left him just enough time to dash by train to Liverpool and embark on the SS *Laurentic*, due to sail for Quebec the next day.

The *Montrose* had a three-day lead but was still 11 days out from Quebec. With a speed of 13 knots the *Laurentic* could easily overtake the *Montrose*. Reaching the St Lawrence River first, Dew disguised himself as a tug pilot and boarded the ship. He walked up to Crippen, shook his hand and removed his pilot's cap saying, 'Good afternoon Dr Crippen, remember me? I'm Inspector Dew with Scotland Yard.' Staring at the inspector in total disbelief Crippen replied, 'Thank God it's over' and held out his wrists for the handcuffs.

As a result of this incident the number of ships fitted with wireless rose dramatically. Dr Crippen was taken back to England, tried for murder and hanged on 28 November 1910 in London.

During World War I the SS *Laurentic* met a tragic end. In 1914 she was selected by the British Admiralty as a transport vessel. On 25 January 1917 she called at Lough Swilly, Ireland,

S.S. "LAURENTIC."

HORS D'ŒUVRES VARIES

PUREE OF SPLIT PEAS   CONSOMME OLGA

STEAMED LITTLE NECK CLAMS

PLAIN & SAVOURY OMELETTES—TO ORDER

VEAL AND HAM PIE
CORNED PORK, BOSTON BAKED BEANS

BAKED JACKET & MASHED POTATOES
TO ORDER FROM THE GRILL. (10 Min).
BORDEAUX SQUABS
SIRLOIN STEAKS & RING ONIONS
STRAW POTATOES
THE BUFFET—
FRESH OYSTERS   SARDINES   DRESSED CRAB
MAYONNAISE OF FRESH SALMON

SIRLOIN OF BEEF   ROAST CHICKEN
LEICESTERSHIRE PIE
HOME-MADE BRAWN   BRAISED BEEF A LA GELEE
BOAR'S HEAD WITH PISTACHIOS
CORNED OX TONGUE   BRAISED YORK HAM
LAMB, MINT SAUCE   GALANTINE OF TURKEY

LETTUCE   BEETROOT   TOMATOES
FRENCH & MAYONNAISE DRESSING

APPLE TART
CEREALINE CUSTARD PUDDING   PASTRY

AMERICAN ICE CREAM

CHEESE—CHESHIRE, CAMEMBERT, STILTON, GORGONZOLA
CANADIAN ST IVEL GRUYERE GOUDA

DESSERT   COFFEE

JUNE 27TH 1911

on her way from Liverpool to discharge four sailors who had become ill, and then continued her passage to deliver cargo to Nova Scotia for the Canadian and American governments, as payment for munitions. However, 45 minutes after leaving Ireland she was struck by two mines laid by a German U-boat. She sank within an hour. A bitter winter storm was blowing at the time of the tragedy and many of the sailors froze to death trying to reach shore. A total of 315 sailors survived.

The *Laurentic*'s cargo contained 3,200 gold bars. Between 1917 and 1924 a number of British Navy salvage operations recovered the bodies of dead seamen and most of the gold bars from the wreck. However, it is generally believed that the ship's safe still contains up to 25 gold bars, worth about £30 million.

Unusually for a liner of the time, the menu is in English, not French, perhaps for the benefit of American and Canadian passengers. The *Laurentic* could accommodate 1,660 passengers in three classes and was built specifically to travel on the North Atlantic routes. There are some specifically US references in the menu, such as little neck clams (soft shell clams) and squabs (pigeons), as well as American ice cream.

Luggage labels of the period from the White Star Line.

Dr Crippen and Ethel Le Neve are led off the SS Montrose *at Quebec after their capture.*

1912

THE *TITANIC* MENU
A Poignant Memento

On 10 April 1912, the *Titanic*, the largest ship afloat, left Southampton, England on her maiden voyage to New York City. The menu shown is the lunch menu for 14 April, the day she struck an iceberg and sank.

The White Star Line had spared no expense in assuring her luxury, making the liner a legend even before she sailed. Her passengers were a mixture of the world's wealthiest, basking in the elegance of first-class accommodation, and immigrants packed into steerage.

The *Titanic* was touted as the safest ship ever built, so safe that she had been fitted with only 20 lifeboats – enough to provide accommodation for only half her 2,200 passengers and crew. This discrepancy rested on the belief that since the ship's construction made her 'unsinkable', her lifeboats were necessary only to rescue survivors of other sinking ships. Moreover, lifeboats took up valuable deck space.

Four days into her journey, at 11:40 pm on the night of 14 April, she struck an iceberg. Her fireman compared the sound of the impact to 'the tearing of calico, nothing more'. However, the collision was fatal and the icy water soon poured into the ship.

It became obvious that many would not find room in a lifeboat. Each passenger was issued with a life jacket but life expectancy would be short when exposed to water four degrees below freezing. As the forward portion of the ship sank deeper, passengers scrambled to the stern. John Thayer witnessed the sinking from a lifeboat. 'We could see groups of the almost fifteen hundred people still aboard, clinging in clusters or bunches, like swarming bees; only to fall in masses, pairs or singly, as the great aft part of the ship, two hundred and fifty feet of it, rose into the sky, till it reached a sixty-five or seventy degree angle.' The great ship slowly slid beneath the waters two hours and forty minutes after the collision

The next morning, the liner *Carpathia* rescued 705 survivors. One thousand five hundred and twenty-two passengers and crew were drowned. The subsequent inquiry attributed the high loss of life to the insufficient number of lifeboats on board and inadequate training in their use.

R.M.S. "TITANIC

APRIL 14, 1912.

LUNCHEON.

CONSOMMÉ FERMIER   COCKIE LEEKIE
FILLETS OF BRILL
EGG À L'ARGENTEUIL
CHICKEN À LA MARYLAND
CORNED BEEF, VEGETABLES, DUMPLINGS

FROM THE GRILL.
GRILLED MUTTON CHOPS
MASHED, FRIED & BAKED JACKET POTATOES

CUSTARD PUDDING
APPLE MERINGUE   PASTRY
BUFFET.
SALMON MAYONNAISE   POTTED SHRIMPS
NORWEGIAN ANCHOVIES   SOUSED HERRINGS
PLAIN & SMOKED SARDINES
ROAST BEEF
ROUND OF SPICED BEEF
VEAL & HAM PIE
VIRGINIA & CUMBERLAND HAM
BOLOGNA SAUSAGE   BRAWN
GALANTINE OF CHICKEN
CORNED OX TONGUE

LETTUCE   BEETROOT   TOMATOES
CHEESE.
CHESHIRE, STILTON, GORGONZOLA, EDAM,
CAMEMBERT, ROQUEFORT, ST. IVEL.
CHEDDAR

Iced draught Munich Lager Beer 3d. & 6d. a Tankard.

The main dining-room of the SS Titanic. *The largest ship in the world in its day, the* Titanic *sank after hitting an iceberg on its maiden voyage from Southampton, England, to New York in 1912.*

REMINISCENCE OF A SURVIVOR

Elizabeth Shutes' account first appeared in *The Truth About the Titanic,* by Archibold Gracie (1913).

Suddenly a queer quivering ran under me, apparently the whole length of the ship. Startled by the very strangeness of the shivering motion, I sprang to the floor . . . a friend said: 'Come quickly to my cabin; an iceberg has just passed our window; I know we have just struck one' . . .

Not until then, did I realize the horror of an accident at sea. Now it was too late to dress; no time for a waist, but a coat and skirt were soon on; slippers were quicker than shoes; the stewardess put on our life-preservers . . . Now only pale faces, each form strapped about with those white bars. So gruesome a scene. We passed on. The awful good-byes. The quiet look of hope in the brave men's eyes as the wives were put into the lifeboats. Nothing escaped one at this fearful moment. We left from the sun deck, seventy-five feet above the water. Mr Case and Mr Roebling, brave American men, saw us to the lifeboat, made no effort to save themselves, but stepped back on deck. Later they went to an honoured grave. . . . The first touch of our lifeboat on that black sea came to me as a last good-bye to life, and so we put off – a tiny boat on a great sea – rowed away from what had been a safe home for five days . . .

But surely the outline of that great, good ship was growing less. The bow of the boat was getting black. Light after light was disappearing, and now those rough seamen put to their oars and we were told to hunt under seats, any place, anywhere, for a lantern, a light of any kind. Every place was empty. There was no water – no stimulant

of any kind. Not a biscuit – nothing to keep us alive had we drifted long. The stars slowly disappeared, and in their place came the faint pink glow of another day. Then I heard, 'A light, a ship' . . . Someone found a newspaper; it was lighted and held up. Then I looked and saw a ship. A ship bright with lights; strong and steady she waited, and we were to be saved. A straw hat was offered: it would burn longer. That same ship that had come to save us might run us down. But no; she is still. The two, the ship and the dawn, came together, a living painting.

FANCY DRESS FOR DINNER
THE SS *NALDERA*

T hese two menus are from
the P & O liner SS *Naldera*
in 1929 en route to
Singapore, one for breakfast
and one for a fancy-dress
dinner. This is an extract from a letter
written on board on 7 March 1929,
the date of the breakfast menu:

We are nearly in the Straits and after
1,200 miles from Colombo have sighted
land. At 11.30 pm we shall reach Penang
(Malay Peninsula) on the island of Penang
and leave 3 p.m. Friday for Singapore. A lot
of passengers leave at Penang and we are
gradually becoming emptier. There are vari-
ous collections for the seaman's Friends etc
for sports. Men had to contribute 15/- and
women 10/- towards prizes and presents for
Stewards decorating the Salon etc, for fancy
dress dances. Am not dancing much,
although there is one most evenings; it is
too hot and most people are strangers.
The second class seem to have a jollier time,
and with them dinner dress is optional, –
in fact the 1st class is rather stiff, too much
swank in some quarters. Boat rather vibrat-
ing this morning. Has a bit of list on as
piles of mails are being got on deck for
Penang. There are 7,000 bags at
Marseilles of mail.   W. H. Webster.

On the bottom of the breakfast menu it
states that a short notice of interest to
passengers will usually be found overleaf.
There it says that '. . . Pulo Perak should
be passed before dark and the *Naldera* is
expected to berth alongside Penang wharf
about 11.30 pm. Provisional time of
departure 3 pm Friday. Breakfast will be
arranged for passengers leaving by the

P. & O. S.S. "NALDERA."

26th February, 1929

Fancy Dress Dinner.

SOUPS

Clear   Royale
Thick   Ox Tail

FISH

Boiled Salmon, Hollandaise Sauce

JOINTS

Fillet of Beef Piqué
Quarter of Lamb, Mint Sauce

ENTREES

Plover Bardée
Asparagus, Vinaigrette Sauce

POULTRY

Roast Capon & Bacon   Salad

VEGETABLES

Roast and Boiled Potatoes
Green Peas

COLD BUFFET

Roast Beef   Melton Mowbray Pie
York Ham

SWEETS

Panniers des Cerises et Crème
Meringue Chantilly
Vanilla Cream Ices

SAVOURY

Cheese Soufflé

Dessert   Coffee

A photograph taken in 1927 during a fancy-dress ball on the Aquitania *gives the flavour of these occasions. The* Aquitania *ocean liner had one of the largest floating ball-rooms in the world. Here passengers visit the bridge of the luxurious ship during a masked ball attended by 200 couples.*

early train'. This was a good way of keeping the passengers informed. The breakfast menu included Force, an American wheatflakes breakfast cereal of the time. The dinner menu is in a mixture of French and English. The clear soup 'Royale' is a chicken soup garnished with set custard shapes. The joints include fillet of beef *piqué* (spiced). The plover *bardée is* served with its breast covered with bacon or fat to prevent the meat drying out. The sweets include cherries and cream and meringues with sweetened whipped cream: passengers in those days were not expected to worry about their waistlines.

P. & O. S.S. "NALDERA."

7th March, 1929

Breakfast.

Grape Nuts   Force

Quaker Oats
Fried Bream
Grilled Calf's Liver
Sweet Corn Cakes
Broiled Bacon
Tomato Omelet

COLD   York Ham   Ox Tongue
Ribs of Beef

Griddle Cakes
Stewed Apples
Fruit

Iced Tea
                                Iced Coffee

_____

P.T.O.—*A short notice of interest to passengers will usually be found overleaf.*

ELEGANT ART DECO
THE SS *STRATHNAVER*

The SS *Strathnaver* was built by Vickers Armstrong and launched on 5 February 1931, setting off on her maiden voyage from London to Sydney on 2 October. The voyage went without any problems, the liner sailing to Sydney via Marseilles, Suez, Bombay and Colombo.

The striking art deco design for the menu was used at this time for a number of different ships in the P & O fleet. Around the borders of the menu itself there are delicate illustrations of fairies offering up culinary delights. Dinner on board a P & O liner in the 1930s was a grand affair. This menu offered such treats as foie gras 'eclairs' as an hors-d'oeuvre. Eclairs are usually filled with cream and iced with chocolate; here they are stuffed with the rich delicacy of goose liver. There are the usual two soups, clear and thick, and sole cooked in butter. Among the hot dishes, diners are offered hazel grouse, a French woodland variety with a distinctive nutty flavour, and artichoke hearts with butter. The salad is special too – garnished with asparagus tips and sliced truffles. Finally, after the sweets, hot cheese pastries are served as a savoury.

This charming art deco menu commemorates a dinner on board the SS Strathnaver *on 27 August 1932.*

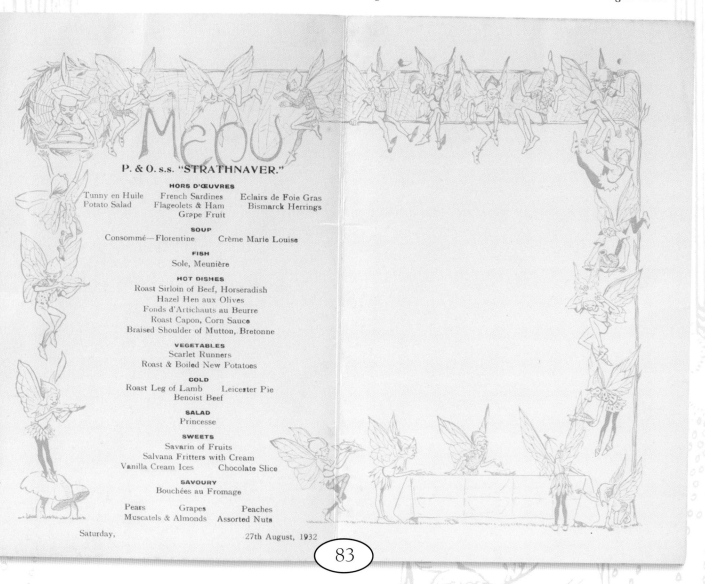

Menu

P. & O. s.s. "STRATHNAVER."

HORS D'ŒUVRES
Tunny en Huile French Sardines Eclairs de Foie Gras
Potato Salad Flageolets & Ham Bismarck Herrings
Grape Fruit

SOUP
Consommé—Florentine Crème Marie Louise

FISH
Sole, Meunière

HOT DISHES
Roast Sirloin of Beef, Horseradish
Hazel Hen aux Olives
Fonds d'Artichauts au Beurre
Roast Capon, Corn Sauce
Braised Shoulder of Mutton, Bretonne

VEGETABLES
Scarlet Runners
Roast & Boiled New Potatoes

COLD
Roast Leg of Lamb Leicester Pie
Benoist Beef

SALAD
Princesse

SWEETS
Savarin of Fruits
Salvana Fritters with Cream
Vanilla Cream Ices Chocolate Slice

SAVOURY
Bouchées au Fromage

Pears Grapes Peaches
Muscatels & Almonds Assorted Nuts

Saturday, 27th August, 1932

STYLISH DINING WITH THE WHITE STAR LINE

THE SS GEORGIC

This menu is for a carnival dinner on board the White Star liner *Georgic*. It was designed as a letter card providing a souvenir of the voyage, a novel idea and a clever piece of advertising. Carnival dinners and fancy-dress dinners were all part of the entertainment provided on these floating palaces.

The SS *Georgic* was built for the Liverpool to New York service by Harland and Wolff at Belfast. She was launched on 12 November 1931 and sailed on her maiden voyage on 25 June 1932. In 1935 she was switched to the Southampton to New York route.

The interior decoration of this ship was distinctive in style, providing the latest and most comfortable of appointments and furnishings. The ship had three classes of passenger: cabin, tourist and third, and catered for the demand for luxury at a reasonable price.

The cuisine was varied and of excellent quality. The dinner included a choice of two soups, beef broth with fried bread squares, and cream of duck soup. The boiled chicken and bacon is served with a thick cream sauce.

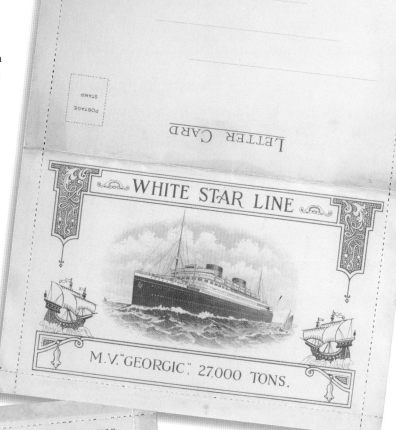

LETTER CARD

POSTAGE STAMP

WHITE STAR LINE

M.V. "GEORGIC" 27,000 TONS.

On board M.V. _____
_____ 193_

Carnival Dinner

M/V "GEORGIC"
May 11th, 1936

MENU

FRUIT COCKTAILS

CROUTE AU POT
CREAM OF DUCKLING, NANTAISE

FRIED FILLETED HAKE, SAUCE TARTARE

OX TAIL SAUTE WITH VEGETABLES

BOILED CHICKEN AND BACON, SUPREME SAUCE

CAULIFLOWER, PARMESAN
PARSNIP FRITTERS
BOILED AND ROAST POTATOES

BUFFET
ROAST LAMB PRESSED BEEF LEICESTER BRAWN
LYON AND SALAMI SAUSAGE

FRENCH PASTRIES
VANILLA ICE CREAM AND WAFERS

APPLES   ORANGES   GRAPES
NUTS ASSORTED

COFFEE   TC

Right: Illustrations from the White Star Line brochure, showing the standard of furnishings and fittings aboard their liners. The liners had three classes, cabin (first), tourist (second) and third. Shown here is the comfortable tourist class bedroom and dining-room and the third class dining-room, designed for large parties. The swimming pool has a modern tiled surround and is designed for onlookers as well as swimmers.

CUNARD WHITE ST

SWIMMING POOL

For a grand pick-me-up, slide into a bathing suit and visit the lovely, modern tiled Swimming Pool, where there is always a gallery of onlookers as gay and care-free as the swimmers themselves. After a few minutes' frolic in the frequently-changed, tangy salt water, you will feel like a new person—and keen to enjoy the entertainments and games in progress, on the sports deck.

"BRITANNIC" & "GEORGIC"

CUNARD WHITE STAR

TOURIST DINING SALOON

A feature of the Tourist Dining Saloon is the provision made for parties travelling together, and tables with seating accommodation ranging from two to eight persons. The walls of the dining saloon are panelled and coloured in various art shades.

"BRITANNIC" & "GEORGIC"

CUNARD WHITE STAR

TOURIST TWO-BERTH ROOM

A notable feature of the Tourist accommodation is the number of well-furnished and airy two-berth staterooms which are available for married couples, or friends desirous of being berthed together. These rooms, which are comfortably spacious, are fitted with two single beds and equipped with hot and cold running water.

"BRITANNIC" & "GEORGIC"

CUNARD WHITE STAR

THIRD CLASS DINING SALOON

Here again, small and large tables are arranged for the convenience of parties travelling together. The panelling and colouring of the walls in the dining saloon are pleasing to the eye. The Company has always been famous for its cuisine, and the table served is no exception to the rule.

"BRITANNIC" & "GEORGIC"

CUNARD WHITE STAR

MAIDEN VOYAGE TO NEW YORK

RMS QUEEN MARY

"Merrie England." Painting by Philip Connard, R.A., R.W.S., in the Restaurant, R.M.S. "Queen Mary."

Cunard White Star

Above: Cover of the menu served the day after the Queen Mary *reached New York. It shows one of the original paintings hung in the restaurant.*

On 27 May 1936 the *Queen Mary* set out from Southampton on her maiden voyage to the US. She arrived in New York on 1 June, and this menu is for dinner on 2 June when she was docked in New York harbour.

At Southampton the weather was good as a seemingly endless stream of passengers, cabin trunks and stewards boarded the ship. Among those aboard for the historic first crossing were Rose Kennedy, wife of the American Ambassador Joseph P. Kennedy, and the designer Cecil Beaton. The upper decks were full of excitement as friends and family bade farewell to one another. The ship exuded elegance: the art deco splendour and graceful lines were something to behold.

A tug slowly guided her out of the harbour, with thousands of cheering people waving goodbye. By late afternoon she arrived in Cherbourg harbour, where she was greeted by a flotilla of ships anxious to witness this historic event. Here more passengers boarded the ship en route to New York.

During her maiden voyage, and throughout her life, the *Queen Mary* played host to many of the world's richest and most famous people: European aristocrats, American business tycoons and Hollywood stars all sailed aboard the *Queen Mary*.

The passengers enjoyed an array of activities such as squash, deck games and strolls around the deck, while the food was the finest money could buy. The ship boasted 'the largest à la carte restaurant' (see page 88) and guests marvelled at the chef's daily creations. In addition, the 'floating city' housed all the necessities found ashore. There were two chapels, a synagogue, a hospital, nurseries and playrooms for the children. It was also possible

DINER

VINS

Caviar de Beluga

Tortue Claire au Xérès

Suprême de Sole, Queen Mary

Maxwell's Amontillado

Poussin en Cocotte Belle Meunière
Petits Pois Frais   Pommes Croquettes
Salade Louise

Chateau Coutet
(Chateau Bottled), 1922
Berncasteler Auslese
Gold Label (Sichel), 1933

Aspérges en Branches Sauce Divine

Fraises frappées Romanoff
Petits Fours

Pommery & Greno Nature, 1926

Coupes glacées Nesselrode

Corbeille de Fruits

Bisquit Dubouché, 1865
Liqueurs

Café

Tuesday, June 2nd, 1936

for passengers to make hotel reservations ashore with a ship-to-shore call.

On the morning of 1 June the *Queen Mary* sailed past the Ambrose Channel light ship, which marked the beginning of the channel into the Hudson river. The reception she received when she reached New York was no less grand than had been the send-off from England. As the majestic liner approached New York she was met by a fleet of vessels representing the Navy, the Coast Guard and local ferry companies, with fire service boats spouting their water hoses, making a series of fountains along the river. Meanwhile planes circled above in tribute. Swarms of Americans clamoured to get a first glimpse of her elegant silhouette. Overcrowded ferries sailed alongside the ship while smaller boats darted recklessly in and out of the harbour traffic. Bands played, music blared and the boats all blew their horns continuously. All in all, it was quite a scene.

The menu is suitably luxurious for such a great occasion, including Beluga caviar (considered the best), turtle soup, asparagus, and chestnut ice cream pudding.

THE BUILDING OF THE RMS *QUEEN MARY*

The Cunard company began planning a new liner in 1926. John Brown & Co of Clydebank were chosen as shipbuilders in May 1930, and work began on Job No 534, as it was known. But in 1931 work was halted because of the Great Depression, with Cunard unable to secure further bank loans; 9,000 men were dismissed from the shipyard. This was a disaster for Clydeside as well as Cunard. Pressure was put on the Government to help, and in the end the Treasury agreed to loan £4,500,000 towards completion.

In April 1934 the workers were given back their jobs and construction resumed. The ship was completed in September 1934 and launched by Queen Mary. In March the *Queen Mary* left the shipyard. Official speed trials were held off the Isle of Arran and then on 12 May 1936 the ship was officially handed over to Cunard. On 25 May a royal party came to visit the ship, including King Edward VIII, Queen Mary, Princess Elizabeth (the present Queen) and the Duke and Duchess of York, soon to be King and Queen.

MENU

Caviar

Clear Turtle Soup with
Sherry

Fillet of Sole

Casserole of Baby
Chicken
Fresh Peas
Potato Croquettes
Salad

Asparagus in Sauce

Strawberries
Fancy Biscuits

Chestnut Ice Cream
Sundae

Basket of Fruit

Coffee

Above: The sumptuous main restaurant on the
Queen Mary, *which could seat nearly 800 diners.*

On the back of the menu one diner jotted down some memorable phrases from the after-dinner speeches:

'expressed pleasure at this great chunk of England tied to an American dock'

'may the great and lasting friendship between the British Empire and America last forever'

welcome could not be surpassed'

'while Britain loves the sea and has seamen to build ships for her'

C. R. Hoffmann,
Southampton
1260   CUNARD WHITE STAR LINER "QUEEN MARY." THE WORLD'S LARGEST LINER.
LENGTH 1,018 FT. HEIGHT FROM MAST-HEAD TO WATER-LINE 250 FT. FROM TOP OF FUNNELS TO WATER-LINE 130 FT. TONNAGE 80,773.
SPEED EXCEEDING 30 KNOTS. THE LARGEST AND FASTEST SHIP IN THE WORLD. ACCOMMODATION FOR 5,000 PASSENGERS.
LAUNCHED AT CLYDEBANK BY HER MAJESTY THE QUEEN. 26TH SEPTEMBER, 1934.

THE QUEEN MARY AT WAR

The *Queen Mary* was crossing the Atlantic to New York with a full complement of passengers when war was declared in September 1939. She finished the voyage following a wild zigzag pattern intended to confuse any German U-boats in the vicinity. For a time she languished at the New York pier, painted a drab grey, alongside the French line's *Normandie*. Then in March 1940 she received orders to sail for Sydney to be outfitted for trooping duties. Many of the ornate fixtures were removed and armaments added, such as anti-aircraft cannons, rocket launchers and a central gun-control house.

At Sydney the remainder of the luxury fittings were removed and she was fitted with berths to accommodate 5,500 troops: her speed and size made her ideally suited for transport duties. She departed on her first voyage on 5 May 1940, part of a convoy responsible for transporting Australian troops from Sydney to Gourock on the Clyde in Scotland. She then sailed back to Sydney for another load of troops, and so on until the US entry into the war in December 1941.

Once America had entered the war, the ship was assigned to ferry American troops to Australia to boost the country's defences against the anticipated Japanese invasion. The *Queen Mary* sailed to Boston where her troop capacity was increased to 8,500 and she was fitted with heaver calibre guns and antiaircraft cannons. Soon she was reassigned to the Atlantic, ferrying GIs to the European front. Prime Minister Winston Churchill later credited the *Queens* – *Queen Mary* and *Queen Elizabeth* – with shortening the war by one year through this effort. In all she logged nearly 600,000 miles (965,580km) and transported over 750,000 troops. One little-known fact is that Winston Churchill himself made three trips on the *Queen Mary* during the war to attend war conferences in the US.

Following the armistice in 1945, the *Queen Mary* was switched to returning US troops to America. The end of the war in Europe meant that there was an urgent need to redeploy thousands of combat troops to the conflict in the Pacific and the Far East. In January 1946 she began the process of taking GI brides to America.

In September 1946 the *Queen Mary* was finally released from military service and returned to Southampton for a complete refit, lasting ten months, that would return her to her pre-war glory.

Saumon Mayonnaise, Truite Saumonée Froide, Cailles à la Bordeaux, Canetons de Rouen à l'Archiduc, Les Poulets Gras au Cresson, Langue de Boeuf Fumée, Parfait de Foie Gras, Les Épinards aux Croûtons, Jambon de Bayonne, Oeufs de Pluviers, Gelée d'Oranges, Petits Savarins au Kirsch, Meringues à la Chantilly, Bûche de Noël, Tête de Veau en Tortue, Petite Marmite, Salade de Homard, Barquettes d'Écrevisses, Salmis de Gelinottes, Riz de Veau, Filets de Sole Mornay, Canetons à la Suprême de Volaille aux Truffes, Turbot Sauce Hollandaise, Oeufs de Pluviers, Haricots Verts, Filet de Boeuf, Chapon du Mans, Bombe Glacée, Gelée Noël, Potage à la Tortue, Consommé Claire, Crême de Riz à la Polonaise, Écrevisses, Saumon Mayonnaise, Truite Saumonée Froide, Cailles à Canetons de Rouen à l'Archiduc, Les Poulets Gras au Cresson, Langue Oeufs de Pluviers, Parfait de Foie Gras, Les Épinards aux Croûtons, Ja Glacée, Gelée d'Oranges, Petits Savarins au Kirsch, Meringues à la Ch à la PolonaiseTête de Veau en Tortue, Petite Marmite, Salade de Hom Cailles à la Bordeaux, Salmis de Gelinottes, Riz de Veau, Filets de Sole de Boeuf Fumée, Suprême de Volaille aux Truffes, Turbot Sauce Hol Jambon de Bayonne, Haricots Verts, Filet de Boeuf, Chapon du Man Chantilly, Bûche de Noël, Potage à la Tortue, Consommé Claire, Crê Homard, Barquettes d'Écrevisses, Saumon Mayonnaise, Truite Saumon Sole Mornay, Canetons de Rouen à l'Archiduc, Les Poulets Gras au Cr Hollandaise, Oeufs de Pluviers, Parfait de Foie Gras, Les Épinards au Mans, Bombe Glacée, Gelée d'Oranges, Petits Savarins au Kirsch, M Crême de Riz à la PolonaiseTête de Veau en Tortue, Petite Marmit Saumonée Froide, Cailles à la Bordeaux, Salmis de Gelinottes, Riz de u Cresson, Langue de Boeuf Fumée, Suprême de Volaille aux Truffes, aux Croûtons, Jambon de Bayonne, Haricots Verts, Filet de Boeuf, C Meringues à la Chantilly, Bûche de Noël, Suprême de Volaille aux

Birthdays and Celebrations

This chapter contains menus of banquets or dinners for a particular person

or occasion. Several are birthday celebrations, from the 87th anniversary of

the birth of the US Civil War hero and later president, Ulysses S. Grant, to

the Diamond Jubilee of Mamie Eisenhowser at the Washington Hilton, and

the 80th birthday celebration for Yehudi Menuhin given at Buckingham

Palace by Prince Charles. Several have a war theme: the lunch at the

Mansion House in London celebrating the anniversary of the US entry into

World War 1, the re-union dinner at the Hotel Cecil for the Independent

Force of the Royal Air Force in 1921, the New Year dinner at Quaglino's

in 1939 with the theme of 'Victory and Peace', and the Victory Day dinner at

the Dorchester in 1946 for all living holders of the Victoria Cross.

ULYSSES S. GRANT

PRESIDENT AND CIVIL WAR HERO

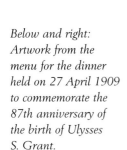

This menu, designed to celebrate the 87th anniversary of the birth of General Ulysses S. Grant, is decorated with scenes from the American Civil War where Grant achieved his famous military victories.

Born in 1822, Grant was raised on a farm and then studied at West Point military academy. After serving in the Mexican War he resigned from the army, but at the outbreak of the Civil War in 1860 he was appointed to command a volunteer regiment. After winning his famous battles against the Confederate Army at Shiloh, Vicksburg and Chattanooga, Abraham Lincoln appointed him general-in-chief in March 1864. He went on to conduct the Wilderness Campaign and devised the strategy that led to the defeat of the Confederate Army, accepting the surrender of General Robert E. Lee at Appomattox on 9 April 1865.

Hailed a hero of the Union, he was made a full general in 1866 and was then nominated Republican candidate for the presidency. He duly became President of the United States in 1869. Although his administration could not be regarded as a success, he was re-elected in 1872 and finally retired in 1877.

Mrs Emma Dent Casey of Washington, sister-in-law of President Grant, gives a fascinating account of his inauguration in *The Sunday Star*, 4 March 1917:

The 4th of March 1869 was typical of Inauguration day. The morning broke gloomily with lowering skies and occasional showers, which later settled into a steady drizzle. The streets were filled with a hurrying crowd moving toward Pennsylvania Avenue. We drove to the north entrance of the Capitol and were escorted to the Senate gallery. Below us on the Senate floor was gathered an imposing sight that grew more impressive with each passing moment. I was awed into hushed expectancy. Into this gathering of senators, the Supreme Court of the United States entered, wearing their sombre official robes. Then General Grant and Vice President Colfax entered, each escorted by a member of the Senate. The general was not in uniform but wore a black suit much to the disgust, so I heard later, of a noted painter, who would portray the general a la General Washington, in all his brave trappings of war, taking the oath of office. No doubt you have often seen copies of this same painting. After this several speeches were made, to which I did not listen. Then General Grant appeared and approached Chief Justice Chase to receive the oath of office. During the war I had been within the dread sound of cannon fire, but never before had it sounded as music to me. Now, the cheering and handclapping and booming of cannon was quite deafening. However dreary the day, there was a wild song of joy in my heart.

Below and right: Artwork from the menu for the dinner held on 27 April 1909 to commemorate the 87th anniversary of the birth of Ulysses S. Grant.

AMERICUS
REPUBLICAN CLUB

1822
GENERAL ULYSSES S·GRANT
1909

MENU

Olives, Celery, Nuts

Clear Turtle Soup with
Madeira

Trout in Butter
Cucumbers

Braised Sweetbreads in a
Tarragon and Wine Vinegar
Sauce
Peas

Fillet of Beef, Coated in Egg
and Breadcrumbs, Cooked
in Butter and Garnished
with Truffles
Potatoes

Kirsch Sorbet

Roast Pigeon
Asparagus with Vinaigrette
Sauce

Strawberries and
Vanilla Ice Cream

*Shown here are pages from
General Grant's commemoration
dinner menu, 27 April 1909.
The menu is illustrated with
highlights from some of Grant's
famous battles during the Civil
War, particularly the Vicksburg
Campaign, the hotly contested
struggle for control of the
Mississippi river.*

MENU

BLUE POINTS

OLIVES   CELERY   SALTED NUTS

GREEN TURTLE CLEAR AU MADEIRA

BROOK TROUT SAUTE MEUNIERE
CUCUMBERS

BRAISED SWEETBREADS BEARNAISE
PETIT POIS

FILET MIGNON A LA RICHELIEU
POMMES BERMUDA

SORBET AU KIRSCH

ROAST PHILADELPHIA SQUAB
NEW ASPARAGUS   SAUCE VINAIGRETTE

STRAWBERRIES AND VANILLA ICE CREAM
ASSORTED CAKES

CHEESE

COFFEE

The dinner to honour Grant's life was given by the Americus Republican Club, Pittsburgh, on 27 April 1909 at the Hotel Schenley. The Schenley was Pittsburgh's finest hotel and attracted visitors of the highest calibre, including Presidents, film stars and sporting heroes. Opened in 1898 it was lavishly decked out with an interior of marble, chandeliers and Louis XV-style architecture. A fitting setting for a banquet to honour a great man.

The dinner began with Blue Points, which are fine oysters from Long Island much favoured by Queen Victoria. It was a rich, elaborate dinner with a liqueur sorbet in the middle to aid digestion. Squab is a young pigeon.

Officers

JOHN DIMLING, PRESIDENT

CHARLES STEWART, VICE PRESIDENT

GEORGE S. HOUGHTON, RECORDING SECRETARY

THOMAS D. GRAHAM, CORRESPONDING SECRETARY

CHARLES E. SCHUETZ, TREASURER

PETER S. COOMBS, RESIDENT SECRETARY

Banquet Committee

GEORGE W. McCANDLESS, CHAIRMAN

THOMAS M. REES, VICE CHAIRMAN

J. HARRY LETSCHE, SECRETARY

HARRY M. LAUGHLIN, TREASURER

JOHN B. BARBOUR, JR.

COL. ALBERT J. LOGAN

EDWARD H. SWINDELL

Reception Committee

WILLIAM McCONWAY, CHAIRMAN

HON. W. H. GRAHAM   A. C. SHAW

COL. J. M. SHOONMAKER   D. L. GILLESPIE

HON. W. A. MAGEE   H. M. LANDIS

JOHN C. DILWORTH   FRANCIS L. ROBBINS

HORACE HAYS   COL. AZOR R. HUNT

TOASTMASTER

HON. PHILANDER C. KNOX

SECRETARY OF STATE

"THE REPUBLICAN PARTY"

HON. CHARLES NAGEL

SECRETARY OF COMMERCE AND LABOR

"GRANT"

HON. DAVID J. FOSTER

MEMBER OF CONGRESS OF VERMONT

"THE ASIATIC QUESTION
AS CALIFORNIANS SEE IT"

HON. DUNCAN E. McKINLAY

MEMBER OF CONGRESS OF CALIFORNIA

LONDON HONOURS A GREAT CHEF

AUGUSTE ESCOFFIER

Escoffier is the best known of all the famous French chefs. In the course of a career lasting 62 years he reached the peak of his profession, as shown by this Jubilee Dinner in his honour at the Monico Restaurant, London, on 23 October 1909. One of the guests was the French President, Armand Fallières.

He began his career at the age of 13, in his uncle's restaurant in Nice. It was a rigorous training, but it stood him in good stead in the years to come. Escoffier came to England in 1890 to join César Ritz in what proved to be a brilliant partnership, Escoffier as Head of Restaurant Services and Ritz as General Manager, first at the Savoy and later at the Ritz and Carlton Hotels, where his fame reached its highest peak. The great French chef Carême had earlier created the concept of *haute cuisine*, but it was Escoffier who modernized and codified it. As a reward for all he had done to enhance the prestige of French cuisine, he was made a Chevalier of the Legion of Honour in 1920.

Larousse Gastronomique, the French cookery bible, tells a famous story: Just before World War I, the German Emperor Wilhelm II attended a banquet on the liner *Imperator*, where Escoffier had taken charge of the imperial kitchens. The Emperor, congratulating him, said, 'I am the Emperor of Germany, but you are the Emperor of chefs.' The best known of his original dishes is Pêche Melba, his tribute to the great Australian singer Dame Nellie Melba at a dinner in her honour in 1893, when she was staying at the Carlton Hotel.

The menu at this dinner is fairly simple, but no doubt it was all perfectly cooked. It must have been nerve-wracking for the chef of the restaurant, producing a meal for this chef of chefs. The most complicated dish is the baked fillet of sole, created by Dugléré, a pupil of the famous chef Carême.

The menu for the Jubilee Dinner in honour of Escoffier, held at the Monico Restaurant, London, on 23 October 1909.

.. Menu ...

Whitstable Native

* . *

Filets de Sole à la Dugléré

* . *

Poularde en Casserole Paysanne

* . *

Viandes froides —

Jambon d'York à la Gelée
Filet de Boeuf à la Russe
Langue de Boeuf fumée
Terrine de Lièvre aux Truffes
Hure de Sanglier aux Pistaches
Pressed Beef à l'Anglaise
Salade Lorette

* . *

Bombe glacée Pralinée
Friandises

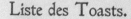

Liste des Toasts.

à sa MAJESTE EDOUARD VII.

à Monsieur FALLIERES, Président de la République
Française.
Par le Président.

à Monsieur AUG. ESCOFFIER : Par le Président.
Réponse de Monsieur Escoffier.

à Monsieur ESCOFFIER, au nom de la Jeunesse
Culinaire.
Par Mons. Jean Roy.

à Monsieur ESCOFFIER, au nom du Salon Culinaire
Par Mons. Gaston Sévin.

à Monsieur ESCOFFIER, au nom de la Société
Technique de l'Alimentation.
Par Mons. Joseph Abrazard.

Aux Invités et aux Délégations Parisiennes,
Par Mons. Emile Fetu.

Aux Souscripteurs,   Par Mons. Paul Corroyer

à la Presse.   Par Mons. Auguste Espèzel.

MENU

Oysters

Fillet of Sole, Baked on a Layer of
Tomatoes and Herbs with a Wine
and Cream Sauce

Chicken Casserole with
Vegetables

COLD DISHES
Glazed York Ham
Fillet of Beef in Madeira-
Flavoured Aspic, Garnished with
Eggs, Stuffed Artichoke Hearts
and Lettuce
Smoked Tongue
Terrine of Hare with Truffles
Wild Boar's Head with Pistachios
Pickled Boiled Beef, Pressed and
Sliced, in Aspic
Salad of Lamb's Lettuce, Grated
Celeriac and Cooked Beetroot

Moulded Ice Cream, Decorated
with Crushed Praline
Pastries and Sweetmeats

SOME DISHES CREATED BY ESCOFFIER

Pêche Melba, for Nellie Melba, the Australian opera singer. Peeled peaches macerated in vanilla syrup on top of a thick layer of vanilla ice cream. The peaches are then covered with raspberry purée.

Cuisses de Nymphe Aurore, for Edward Prince of Wales. Meaning 'legs of the dawn nymph', this is a dish of frogs' legs.

Tournedos Rossini, for the famous composer. Medallion of beef fillet sautéed in butter and placed on a fried bread round. A slice of foie gras sautéed in butter is placed on top and then slices of truffle, tossed in the meat cooking juices.

Chaudfroid Jeannette, named after the ship *Jeannette* which became ice-bound on an expedition to the North Pole. Boned, poached chicken, coated and glazed with a rich white sauce and served cold.

Réjane Salad, for the famous actress Gabrielle Réju. Salad of potato, asparagus tips, as well as sliced truffles.

Rachel Mignonettes of Quail, for the famous dramatic actress Rachel Félix. Small pieces of grilled quail, served on artichoke hearts and topped with grilled slices of bone marrow. Served with a red wine sauce.

TO KEEP UP MORALE
POW Camp Gütersloh, Germany

All prisoners of war dream of food, and never more so than at Christmas and New Year, when they think of the celebrations they could have been enjoying. This fantasy menu was handwritten during World War 1 by a prisoner in the German prisoner-of-war camp at Gütersloh, New Year's Eve 1917, presumably to keep up the morale of his fellow prisoners. The cover shows a drawing of the insignia of his regiment, and inside is the menu he would have liked in different circumstances.

Gütersloh is in western Germany, between Hanover and Düsseldorf. The camp is now run by the British Army, as part of the official British Force in Germany, and is attended by school and army cadets for training purposes.

Although dated New Year's Eve, the menu is much more what you would expect for Christmas dinner – perhaps they had all spent the previous week talking about their favourite Christmas dishes.

The menu for the fantasy dinner at POW Camp Gütersloh, New Year's Eve, 1917, signed by some of the would-be diners.

Above: A drawing of the prisoner's regimental insignia.

Menu.

Consommé.

Fried Sole.
Boiled Potatoes.

Roast Turkey.
Baked Potatoes
Beetroot
French Beans.

Xmas Pudding.
Cream.

Preserved Fruits.

Coffee.

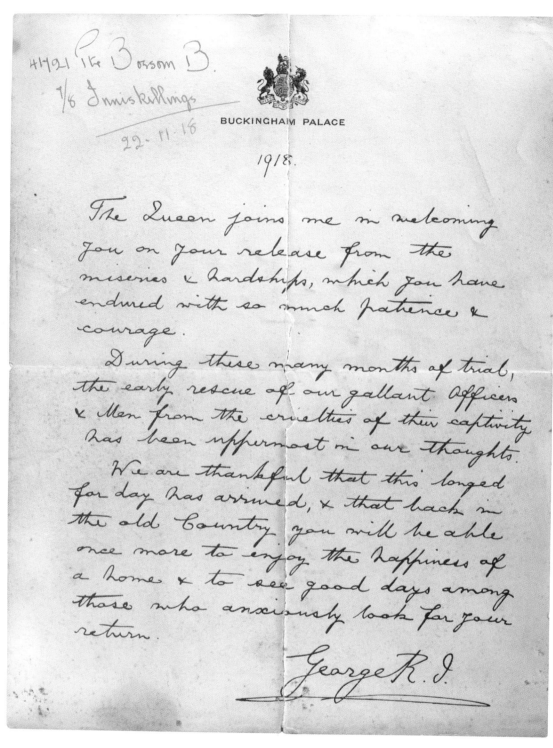

BUCKINGHAM PALACE

1918.

The Queen joins me in welcoming you on your release from the miseries & hardships, which you have endured with so much patience & courage.

During these many months of trial, the early rescue of our gallant Officers & Men from the cruelties of their captivity has been uppermost in our thoughts.

We are thankful that this longed for day has arrived, & that back in the old Country you will be able once more to enjoy the happiness of a home & to see good days among those who anxiously look for your return.

George R.I.

When the war ended, King George V sent messages to the former prisoners of war. One such message, to Pte Bossom, 7/8 Inniskillings, is shown here and transcribed below.

The Queen joins me in welcoming you on your release from the miseries and hardships you have endured with so much patience and courage. During these many months of trial, the early rescue of our gallant officers and men from the cruelties of their captivity has been uppermost in our thoughts. We are thankful that this longed for day has arrived and that back in the old country you will be able once more to enjoy the happiness of a home and to see good days among those who anxiously look for your return.

   George R V

FOR AMERICAN SUPPORT IN WAR

CELEBRATING THE ANNIVERSARY OF THE US ENTRY INTO WORLD WAR 1

A lunch was held at the Mansion House in London on 6 April 1918, the anniversary of the entry of the US into the war. Many distinguished guests were present, including Winston Churchill MP (Minister of Munitions) and Vice-Admiral Sims of the US Navy.

World War I had begun in 1914, and at first America was determined to stay out of the conflict, President Wilson officially declaring US neutrality. But from the start American sympathies were with the Allies, and what tipped the balance in the end was German submarine warfare. France and England had imposed a shipping blockade on Germany, creating an economic stranglehold. Germany tried to break this by using mines and submarines, many American lives being lost in the process. When the liner *Lusitania* was torpedoed in 1915, causing many deaths, it resulted in a lot of anti-German sentiment. And once Germany decided on unrestricted U-boat warfare on merchant shipping, to starve Britain out, American involvement was inevitable. The US entered the war on 6 April 1917, President Woodrow Wilson declaring that the US should 'make the world safe for democracy'.

The gigantic task began of converting US industry to a war footing. The first contingent of the American Expeditionary Force arrived in France in June 1917, and within 18 months an army of 4,000,000 men had been raised, half of whom were sent to France.

Meanwhile the US Navy set out to make war on U-boats. Admiral William Sims is best known for his expertise in the design of ships, but it was he who led the crusade against German U-boats. Promoted to Rear Admiral, Sims was sent to coordinate affairs between England and the US. He helped initiate the convoy system which proved to be very

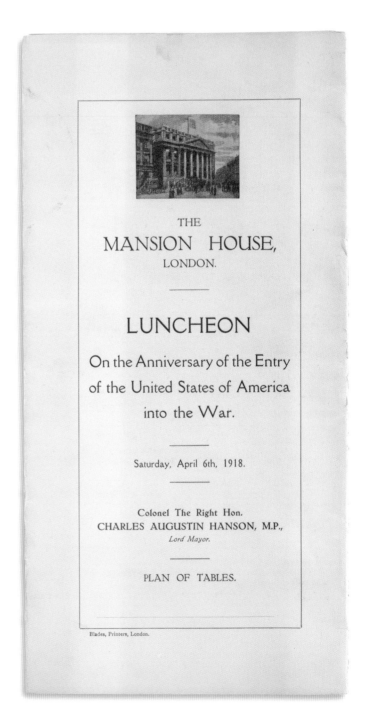

THE
MANSION HOUSE,
LONDON.

LUNCHEON

On the Anniversary of the Entry
of the United States of America
into the War.

Saturday, April 6th, 1918.

Colonel The Right Hon.
CHARLES AUGUSTIN HANSON, M.P.,
Lord Mayor.

PLAN OF TABLES.

Blades, Printers, London.

successful. His plan called for dozens of US destroyers to lead ships across the U-boat-infested waters of the Atlantic. As a result, Secretary Daniels approved a plan that would result in the commissioning of 406 submarine chasers of all classes of ships. By this date in the war US resources of manpower and munitions had altered the picture, and by May US troops were deployed in great numbers along the front. Fighting ended on 11 November 1918.

The menu is mainly in English. Salmon *souché* might mean the fish is thinly sliced and soused (pickled) in brine or vinegar, like soused herring. Whitebait are usually tossed in flour and deep fried. Devilled whitebait probably means that they are tossed in a mixture of flour and hot spices before being fried. Eggs florentine are poached eggs served on a bed of spinach cooked in butter. They are then covered with cheese sauce, sprinkled with grated cheese and browned on top.

MENU.

CLEAR TURTLE.

—

SALMON SOUCHÉ.   CUCUMBER.

—

DEVILLED WHITEBAIT.

—

EGGS FLORENTINE.

—

FRUIT SALADS.
BAKED CUSTARDS.

—

ANCHOVY TOAST.

—

DESSERT.

Admiral William Sims of the United States Navy stands with Assistant Secretary of the Navy Franklin Delano Roosevelt, who later became President, in 1933.

REUNION FOR THE RAF PILOTS

THE INDEPENDENT FORCE, ROYAL AIR FORCE AT THE HOTEL CECIL, LONDON

T he third annual reunion dinner of the Independent Force, Royal Air Force was held at the Hotel Cecil in London in June 1921. In October 1917 Hugh Trenchard, Commander of the Royal Flying Corps in France, had been ordered to commence a strategic bombing campaign against German industrial targets. By early 1918 his squadrons were able to mount the first 'round the clock' bombing raid, against the town of Trier.

In April 1918 the Royal Air Force was formed and it was decided to increase bombing activities. Trenchard was put in charge of this enlarged force, which became known as the Independent Force, RAF, and with it, bombing of the Rhineland towns assumed large dimensions. Trenchard chose to attack as many of the large industrial centres as was possible with the machines at his disposal. Numbers of large bombers equipped for long-distance flying became available and the squadrons of the Independent Force undertook the bombing of the industrial centres of Germany, turning the course of the war.

Signatures on the menu include those of Air-Marshall Trenchard and Wing Commander HRH The Duke of York (later King George VI).

The dinner is traditional hearty fare, though not on the scale of the Edwardians. Crème St Germain is a celebrated French pea soup, made from a purée of fresh peas, clear soup, butter and chervil.

The menu for the third annual reunion dinner of the Independent Force of the Royal Air Force, held at the Hotel Cecil on 20 June 1921. The menu is signed by some of the guests, including the Duke of York (signed Albert) who later became King George VI.

Toast List.

His Majesty the King.
Proposed by—THE CHAIRMAN.

Her Majesty the Queen,
Queen Alexandra, The Prince of Wales,
and the Other Members of the Royal Family.
Proposed by—THE CHAIRMAN.

The Independent Force.
Proposed by—THE CHAIRMAN.
Replied to by—Maj.-Gen. J. E. DICKIE, C.B., C.M.G., and Col. Sir W. R. LAWRENCE, Bart., G.C.I.E., G.C.V.O., C.B.

The Chairman.
Proposed by—Col. Sir W. R. LAWRENCE, Bart., G.C.I.E., G.C.V.O., C.B.
Replied to by—THE CHAIRMAN.

The Secretary of State for Air.
Proposed by—Group-Capt. C. L. N. NEWALL, C.M.G., C.B.E., A.M.
Replied to by—Capt. The Rt. Hon. F. GUEST, C.B.E., D.S.O., M.P.

Menu

Petite Marmite à l'Ancienne
Crème St. Germain

Filet de Sole Newbourg

Medaillon de Bœuf Ninon
Pommes Nouvelles Noisettes

Caneton d'Aylesbury Farci à l'Anglaise
Salade de Laitues aux Œufs

Asperges en Branche, Sauce Hollandaise

Ananas Glace dans son Fruit
Friandises   Gaufrettes

Café

MENU
Clear Broth
Cream of Pea Soup

Fillet of Sole in a
Cream Sauce

Medallion of Beef
Baby New Potatoes
Sautéed in Butter

Stuffed Duck, Poached
in a White Sauce
Lettuce and Egg Salad

Asparagus with Butter
Sauce

Pineapple Ice Cream
Sweetmeats
Wafers
Coffee

WAR IN THE AIR

At the beginning of World War I Britain lacked the capacity to fight a war in the air. Early efforts concentrated on trying to destroy the German Zeppelin airship bases, while frantically developing the fighters and bombers that would eventually win the day through the use of strategic bombing.

British fighter biplanes lined up ready for action at an airfield at Issoudun, France, 1918.

Quaglino's

New Year's Eve

1939-40

HELEN McKIE.

On the cover of the
menu a toast is raised
to the gallant men of
the three services –
Army, Navy and
Air Force.

(stop)

1946

HIGH HONOURS FOR WAR HEROES

VICTORY DAY CELEBRATION AT THE DORCHESTER, LONDON

VICTORY DAY

8th JUNE, 1946

THE DORCHESTER
Park Lane, W.1

A t the end of World War II a Victory Day Celebration Dinner was held at the Dorchester Hotel in London for all living holders of the Victoria Cross. It was attended by 154 VCs.

The Victoria Cross is the highest and most prestigious award for gallantry that can be awarded to British and Commonwealth forces. It was created in 1856 after the Crimean War when it was realized that there was no award open to all ranks. Queen Victoria was closely involved in choosing the design for the cross, which consists of a Maltese cross suspended from a crimson ribbon. The cross is cast from the bronze of cannons captured from the Russians at Sebastopol during the Crimean War. It says simply, 'For Valour'. Since its inception it has been awarded 1,354 times. It has been awarded to the American Unknown Soldier, the reciprocal award of the US Medal of Honour being made to the British Unknown Warrior.

Just one of the 154 Victoria Cross recipients who attended this dinner was Lieutenant Basil Godfrey Place VC, DSO, 1921–94. Place was held in the German naval prison camp

Victory Dinner

Le Fumet de Tortue du Pacifique
en Tasse au Sherry

Le Suprême de Volaille à la Mode de Caen

Les Petites Asperges Anglaises
au Beurre de Normandie

Les Torpilles de la Résistance

Le Biscuit Glacé aux Rubis des
Souverains "Victory"

Le "V" Symbolique

MENU
Pacific Turtle Soup with Sherry

Chicken Breast with
Vegetables in Calvados
English Asparagus with
Normandy Butter
Torpedo-Shaped Potatoes

'Victory' Neapolitan
Ice Cream

Right: The Prince of Wales dines at the House of Lords on 9 November 1929 with holders of the Victoria Cross, representing all parts of the Empire.

Marlag O. He won the Victoria Cross in September 1943 when he commanded the midget submarine X6 in an attack on the German battleship *Tirpitz*. He was unable to escape and was captured.

The menu contains several references to the events of the war: Pacific turtle soup refers to the campaign in the Pacific, *à la Mode de Caen* is a reference to the Normany landings (Caen is a town in Normandy, northern France, which was heavily bombed), as is the Normandy butter with the English asparagus. Resistance torpedoes refers to the French Resistance underground movement.

Right: A contemporary postcard commemorates the founding of the Victoria Cross in 1856, at the end of the Crimean War. It illustrates some of the famous battles in that war and shows the Maltese cross medal with the crimson ribbon.

THE DIAMOND JUBILEE OF A BELOVED FIRST LADY

MAMIE EISENHOWER AT THE WASHINGTON HILTON

The Diamond Jubilee birthday dinner for Mamie Eisenhower was held on 27 September 1976 at the Washington Hilton Hotel, Washington DC. Her husband, the former President Eisenhower, had died in 1969.

Mamie Eisenhower was a very popular First Lady. Her sparkling blue eyes were as well known as Ike's famous grin.

Born in Boone, Iowa, Mamie Geneva Doud moved with her family to Colorado when she was seven. Her father retired from business, and Mamie and her three sisters grew up in a large house in Denver. During winters the family made long visits to relatives in the milder climate of San Antonio, Texas. There, in 1915, at Fort Sam Houston, Mamie met 2nd Lt Dwight D. Eisenhower. Their engagement was announced on Valentine's Day 1916 when Ike gave Mamie his West Point class ring. They were married on 1 July 1916 at the Doud home and cut the wedding cake with Ike's shiny sword.

During more than 50 years of marriage Mamie made home in a bewildering variety of residences: a bat-ridden Panama villa, a Philippine extravaganza, apartments in Paris and Washington, a castle in Scotland, a classical villa at Marne La Coquette, a Morningside Drive mansion, the White House, and finally the Gettysburg farm in Pennsylvania. Their first son Doud Dwight or 'Icky', who was

born in 1917, died of scarlet fever in 1921. A second child, John, was born in 1922 in Denver. Like his father he had a career in the army.

During World War II, while Ike became first Commander of US Forces in Europe and then Supreme Commander of Allied Forces in Europe, Mamie lived in Washington. After the war Ike served as Supreme Commander of Nato, while Mamie took charge of a chateau near Paris. Later, the Eisenhowers retired to their farm at Gettysburg.

The perfect life-long partnership that existed between 'Mamie and Ike' inspired America. At his Inauguration as the 34th President of the United States, as soon as he had spoken the solemn words of the Oath of Office, Ike strode over to Mamie and kissed her. Every previous president had driven back from the Capitol to the White House with his vice-president, but Ike drove back with Mamie beside him in the open car. The Eisenhowers entertained an unprecedented number of heads of state and leaders of foreign governments. Her sincerity and generous, warm-hearted personality not only captivated world leaders but won her a special place of affection in the hearts of people everywhere.

This 'birthday salute' is a symbol of the affection she inspired. The menu is appealing but relatively light, and the guests were entertained by various show business personalities including singer and musical star Ethel Merman.

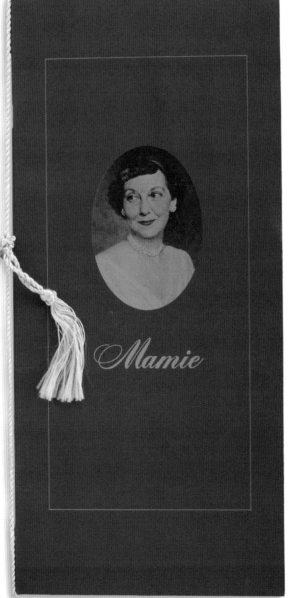

Mamie

Right: Menu and programme for Mamie Eisenhower's birthday salute, held at the Washington Hilton, 27 September 1976.

MENU
Cream of Almond Soup

Celery Hearts with Olives

Beef Medallions with Mushrooms,
Bacon and Diced Potatoes
Puréed Potatoes
Stuffed Artichoke Hearts
Puréed Carrots

Asparagus Tips with Butter

Salad with Palm Hearts, Cherry
Tomatoes, and Strips of Celery, with
Green Goddess Dressing

Maple Jelly

Below: Mamie at the Eisenhower Memorial.

Diamond Jubilee Birthday Salute
to
Mamie Doud Eisenhower

Program

Performers
In order of appearance

Ray Bolger
Master of Ceremonies

Lawrence Welk

Ethel Merman

Red Skelton

Joint Armed Forces
Color Guard

Music

...ine Band

Cream of Almond Soup

Hearts of Celery — Ripe & Green Olives

Tournedos Forestiere
Garnished with Chantrelles & Morilles

Pommes Duchesse

Artichoke Bottoms Farci
with Puree of Carrots

Asparagus Tips au Beurre

Salad Gasconne
with Hearts of Palm, Cherry Tomato
and Julienne of Pascal Celery
Green Goddess Dressing

Maple Mousse

Coffee

TRIBUTE TO AN ARTIST
YEHUDI MENUHIN AT BUCKINGHAM PALACE

MENU

Salad of marinated peppers

• • •

Fillet of turbot and salmon with wild mushrooms
and a champagne sauce

• • •

Cinnamon ice-cream
with spiced poached pears

Thursday, 21st March 1996   Buckingham Palace

On 21 March 1996 Prince Charles, Prince of Wales, invited the great violinist Yehudi Menuhin to Buckingham Palace to celebrate his 80th birthday.

Born in New York in 1916, the son of Russian Jewish immigrants, Yehudi Menuhin had one of the longest and most distinguished careers of any violinist of the 20th century. A child prodigy, he found instant fame at the age of seven with his touching performances of Mendelssohn's Violin Concerto and as a teenager toured the world to great acclaim. As a young man Menuhin studied in Paris under the violinist and composer George Enesco, and during the 1930s he was a much sought-after international performer. During World War II he played in 500 concerts for Allied troops, and after the war was over he returned to Germany to play for those liberated from the concentration camps.

By the 1960s he had increased the scope of his musical involvement. In 1963 he opened the Yehudi Menuhin School in England for musically gifted children. He also began conducting, which he would continue to do until his death. He conducted at many of the important music festivals, and nearly every major orchestra in the world. It was around this time he also broke from his traditional roots and did work other than in classical music. One of his most successful ventures away from traditional performance was with the great Indian composer and sitarist Ravi Shankar. Throughout the last 20 years of his life he continued to work in every aspect of

Above left: Yehudi Menuhin, the famous violinist, at the height of his powers.

music, and as a performer, conductor and teacher he spent his seventies and eighties as one of the most active musicians in the world. He died in Berlin in 1999.

Prince Charles himself plays the cello, and there was a concert for his 21st birthday at Buckingham Palace at which Yehudi Menuhin was invited to play. So it was fitting that Prince Charles should honour the musician's 80th birthday in his turn. The menu is simple but appealing, as befits the occasion and the age of the honoured guest.

WINE LIST

Chassagne-Montrachet 1993, Louis Latour
Corton Domaine Latour Grand Cru 1991

Château Filhot crème de tête 1990

Thursday, 21st March 1996   Buckingham Palace

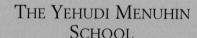
THE YEHUDI MENUHIN SCHOOL

In 1963 Yehudi Menuhin founded this famous music school in Surrey, England. In it he created the perfect conditions in which musically gifted children might develop their potential to the full on stringed instruments and the piano. The school takes 50 pupils, from 8 to 18, and counts Nigel Kennedy the violinist among its illustrious ex-pupils.

After the death of Yehudi Menuhin in 1999 the cellist and conductor Mstislav Rostropovitch was asked to become the new President of the School.

Concert for the opening ceremony of the Anniversary of the Human Rights Declaration at UNESCO, conducted by Yehudi Menuhin, 7 December 1998.

Potage à la Tortue, Consommé Claire, Crème de Riz à la PolonaiseTête
Saumon Mayonnaise, Truite Saumonée Froide, Cailles à la Bordeaux
l'Archiduc, Les Poulets Gras au Cresson, Langue de Boeuf Fumée,
Parfait de Foie Gras, Les Epinards aux Croûtons, Jambon de Bayon
l'Oranges, Petits Savarins au Kirsch, Meringues à la Chantilly, Bûche
de Veau en Tortue, Petite Marmite, Salade de Homard, Barquettes d'E
Salmis de Gelinottes, Riz de Veau, Filets de Sole Mornay, Canetons
Suprême de Volaille aux Truffes, Turbot Sauce Hollandaise, Oeufs de
Haricots Verts, Filet de Boeuf, Chapon du Mans, Bombe Glacée, Gelée
Potage à la Tortue, Consommé Claire, Crème de Riz à la PolonaiseTête
Saumon Mayonnaise, Truite Saumonée Froide, Cailles à la Bordeaux
l'Archiduc, Les Poulets Gras au Cresson, Langue de Boeuf Fumée,
Parfait de Foie Gras, Les Epinards aux Croûtons, Jambon de Bayon
l'Oranges, Petits Savarins au Kirsch, Meringues à la Chantilly, Bûche
de Veau en Tortue, Petite Marmite, Salade de Homard, Barquettes d'E
Salmis de Gelinottes, Riz de Veau, Filets de Sole Mornay, Canetons
Suprême de Volaille aux Truffes, Turbot Sauce Hollandaise, Oeufs de
Haricots Verts, Filet de Boeuf, Chapon du Mans, Bombe Glacée, Gelée
Potage à la Tortue, Consommé Claire, Crème de Riz à la PolonaiseTête
Saumon Mayonnaise, Truite Saumonée Froide, Cailles à la Bordeaux
l'Archiduc, Les Poulets Gras au Cresson, Langue de Boeuf Fumée,
Parfait de Foie Gras, Les Epinards aux Croûtons, Jambon de Bayon
l'Oranges, Petits Savarins au Kirsch, Meringues à la Chantilly, Bûche
de Veau en Tortue, Petite Marmite, Salade de Homard, Barquettes d'E
Salmis de Gelinottes, Riz de Veau, Filets de Sole Mornay, Canetons
Suprême de Volaille aux Truffes, Turbot Sauce Hollandaise, Oeufs de
Haricots Verts, Filet de Boeuf, Chapon du Mans, Bombe Glacée, Gelée

Sporting Events

A number of sporting banquets and dinners have been held over the years. The

menus shown here range from the annual dinner in 1895 of the Thames Rowing

Club, one of the oldest rowing clubs in England, and the University Boat Race

Dinner in 1897, to the British Automobile Racing Club Dinner in 1967, the menu

signed by world champion Graham Hill. More unusual menus include a

charmingly illustrated one for a banquet given by the Aero-Club of France in 1924,

held at the Palais D'Orsay Hotel, Paris, and attended by Louis Blériot, the first

aviator to fly across the Channel, and a British Olympic Association annual dinner

in 1939, just before the outbreak of World War II. There is also a dinner for a now

long-forgotten Women's World Games in 1934, in which 19 countries competed,

battling for the right of women to compete in Olympic track and field events.

THE THAMES ROWING CLUB ANNUAL DINNER

CAFÉ ROYAL, LONDON

I n 1895 the Thames Rowing Club held their annual dinner at the Café Royal, London. The club is based on Putney Embankment, London, and was originally formed in 1860 for 'organized pleasure or exercise rowing'.

The clubhouse was built in 1879, and is a veritable museum of British rowing. The panelled room is lined with commemorative blades, trophies, portraits and so on. In 1895 it was an all-men club of course, but in 1973 it became the first major rowing club to admit women.

The club soon moved into competitive rowing, and since then it has had a successful history at national and international levels, winning nearly every national and international prize of note, and has played a significant role in the development and practice of British rowing.

Rowing has a long history in London. Crossing the Thames by rowing boats was common, and the oarsmen entertained themselves by seeing who could get across in the fastest time. Sculling races were introduced in the early part of the 1700s. Originally boats were heavy and wide, with the oars resting on the side of the boat, but by the mid-1800s outriggers were introduced, allowing the oars to be secured away from the side of the boat. Also the boats became slimmer and more streamlined. Yale University introduced sliding seats in the latter part of the 19th century and these improvements stand to the present day.

The dinner held in 1895 is very typical of the period, and suitable for hearty oarsmen. The boned lark stuffed with truffles is an exotic item, and reminds us how times (and tastes) have changed. Songbirds are protected, being much rarer now, and it would seem like sacrilege to serve them up for dinner, even with truffles.

Above and right: The menu for the Thames Rowing Club Dinner, 2 February 1895, at the Café Royal, London.

The crimson and gilt interior of the Café Royal in London, dating from the 1860s.

MENU

Oysters

Clear Broth
Cream of Cauliflower Soup

Turbot in Butter Sauce
Fillet of Sole in Cheese Sauce

Boned Lark Stuffed with Truffles
Chicken in Tarragon Sauce

Saddle of Mutton with Gooseberry Jelly
Baby Potatoes Sautéed in Butter
Braised Celery

Lobster Mayonnaise

Pheasants and Plovers
Salad

Chilled Mousse

Cheese
Dessert

MENU

Huîtres.

Petite Marmite.   Crème Dubarry.

Turbot, Sauce Hollandaise.
Filets de Soles Mornay.

Mauviettes en Caisses aux Truffes.
Poularde à l'Estragon.

Selle de Mouton, Gelée de Groseilles.
Pommes Noisettes.   Céleri braisé.

Mayonnaise de Homards.

Raisins et Pluviers.
Salade.

Mousse Glacée.

Fromage.   Dessert.

PROGRAMME

Toast - - - - - "The Queen" - - The Chairman.

Toast - - - - - "The Club" - - The Chairman.

Song - - - "Prologue" Pagliacci - Mr. R. Green.

Toast "Other Clubs and Visitors" S. D. Muttlebury.

Song {"Her Golden Hair was hanging down her Back"} Mr. Wilson James.

Song - - - "Venetian Song" Mr. Murray Bemister.

Toast {"The Captain, Hon. Secs and Committee"} F. E. Whitehurst.

Song - - - "Devout Lover" - - - Mr. R. Green.

Song - - "Dandy Coloured Coon" Mr. Wilson James.

Toast "Winning Crews and Coaches" L. H. K. Bushe-Fox.

Song {"Here's a Health unto His Majesty"} Mr. Murray Bemister.

Toast - - - - - "The Press" - - The Chairman.

Pianist - - Mr. Warren Tear.

THE UNIVERSITY BOAT RACE
Café Royal, London

This dinner was given for the crews of the 1897 Oxford and Cambridge Universities Boat Race, held at the Café Royal, London on 3 April 1897. The beautifully hand-painted cover shows the two crews.

The Boat Race takes place on the Thames, between Putney and Mortlake, and is rowed by two teams of eights. The first Boat Race took place in 1829, when Oxford were the winners. It was watched by a crowd of 20,000 people and immediately gained popularity, but for some reason there was not another boat race until 1836 when Cambridge were the victors. The Boat Race has continued regularly ever since, missing only a few years. At the race in 1897 there was a fairly good tide and a breeze, making conditions fast.

Cambridge won the toss and chose the Middlesex station (south bank). By the boathouses Cambridge had half a length's lead, but Oxford caught up quickly. At the Mile Post Cambridge made a concerted effort, but could not sustain it. Oxford were clear at Hammersmith, eventually winning by two and a half lengths in a good time of 19 minutes, 12 seconds.

Even by the standards of the time this was a hearty dinner, suitable for hungry young men who had slaved hard over their oars. The sauce served with the haunch of venison is a traditional peppery game sauce, flavoured with gooseberries. There are some topical references: Sarah Bernhardt was a famous actress of the day, while the Mahdi is a reference to the recent Siege of Khartoum (1885) by the Sudanese forces, when General Gordon was killed.

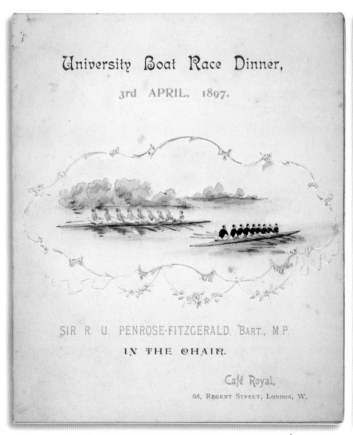

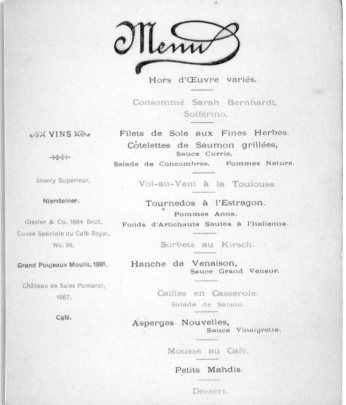

The menu for the 1897 University Boat Race Dinner at the Café Royal, with its hand-painted cover.

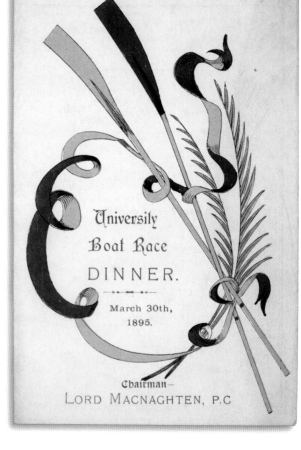

Covers of some previous menus for Boat Race dinners.

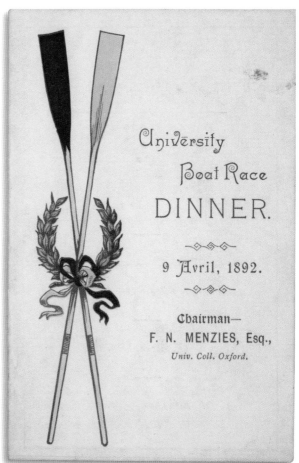

MENU

Hors d'Oeuvres

Clear Soup Garnished with Dumplings,
Crayfish Tails, Tapioca and Beef Marrow
Vegetable Soup with Garlic and Herbs,
Garnished with Chervil and Potato Balls

Fillets of Sole with Mixed Herbs
Grilled Salmon Steaks with Curry Sauce
Cucumber Salad
Boiled Potatoes

Vol-au-Vent with Chicken Dumplings,
Cocks' Combs and Kidneys, Sweetbreads,
Mushrooms and Truffles in Egg Sauce

Beef Medallions with Tarragon Sauce
Potato Cake with Butter
Sautéed Artichoke Hearts in Tomato,
Mushroom and Shallot Sauce

Kirsch Sorbet

Haunch of Venison with Peppery Hunter's
Sauce

Casseroled Quails
Seasonal Salad

Asparagus with Vinaigrette Sauce

Coffee Mousse
Sweet Biscuits
Dessert

BANQUET

Sous la Présidence de

M. Paul PAINLEVÉ

PRÉSIDENT DE LA CHAMBRE DES DÉPUTÉS

donné par

L'AÉRO-CLUB DE FRANCE

En l'honneur des Délégués à la Conférence de Paris

F. A. I.

PALAIS D'ORSAY
Jeudi 26 Juin 1924

THE AÉRO-CLUB OF FRANCE

PALAIS D'ORSAY HOTEL, PARIS

The banquet at the Palais d'Orsay Hotel, Paris in 1924 was given by the Aéro-Club of France. The menu comes with a seating plan, and was attended by such distinguished aviators as Louis Blériot, who made the first Channel crossing by air on 25 July 1909, and Alberto Santos-Dumont, who made the first recorded flight (220 metres) near Paris in 1906.

The Palais d'Orsay Hotel was built in 1898–1900 to coincide with the Paris Exhibition of 1900. One of Paris' most baroque extravaganzas, it had 260 bedrooms and four grand reception rooms. The kitchens were on the sixth floor, as the hotel was on the banks of the Seine, which regularly flooded. The Aéro-Club of France was founded in 1898, when only balloons had flown, not aeroplanes. In due course the Club issued pilot's licences to Orville and Wilbur Wright, the American aviators, Louis Blériot and Alberto Santos-Dumont, who had the first plane in Europe. In 1932 Alberto Santos-Dumont committed suicide. In his final years he had become despondent about the destructive uses of aviation in wartime, and about his role as a pioneer of flight.

The banquet is quite light, perhaps suitable for aviators. A capon is a neutered cock, specially fattened for the table.

MENU
Beef and Vegetable Soup with Croûtons

Cold Salmon Trout in Aspic, Garnished with Truffles and Artichoke Hearts

Ham Garnished with Spinach and Egg in a Cheese Sauce

Spit-Roasted Capon

Salad

Moulded Ice Cream Wafers

Basket of Fruit

BANQUET

SOUS LA PRÉSIDENCE DE

M. PAUL PAINLEVÉ

Président de la Chambre des Députés

donné par

L'AÉRO-CLUB DE FRANCE

en l'honneur des

DÉLÉGUÉS A LA CONFÉRENCE DE PARIS

F. A. I.

◁◁◁◁ *Palais d'Orsay*
Jeudi 26 Juin 1924

MENU

Croûte au pot

Truite saumonée froide à la Parisienne

Jambon de Bayonne à la Florentine

Chapon du Mans à la broche

Salade

Bombe glacée Palais d'Orsay

Gaufrettes

Corbeilles de fruits

⁂

VINS

Médoc-Graves

Beaune

Champagne frappé

Café et Liqueurs

⁂

▷▷▷▷ MUSIQUE ◁◁◁◁

1. *Marche Militaire*............ SAINT-SAËNS
2. *Petite Suite*................ DEBUSSY
3. *Ouverture de la Grotte de Fingal*................ MENDELSSOHN
4. *Au Bal (Valse Lente)*....... E. PESSARD
5. *Les Maîtres Chanteurs (Chant de Concours)*............. WAGNER
6. *Pavane et Rigaudon*........ Louis GANNE
7. *Les Masques (Pulcinelli)*...... PEDROTTI
8. *Lakmé (Sélection)*.......... Léo DELIBES
9. *Madame (La Valse)*......... CHRISTINÉ

Orchestre sous la Direction de M. Hector GUILLET, des Concerts Colonne.
Chef d'Orchestre du Palais d'Orsay.

This whimsical menu was designed for the banquet held on 26 June 1924 by the Aéro-Club of France.

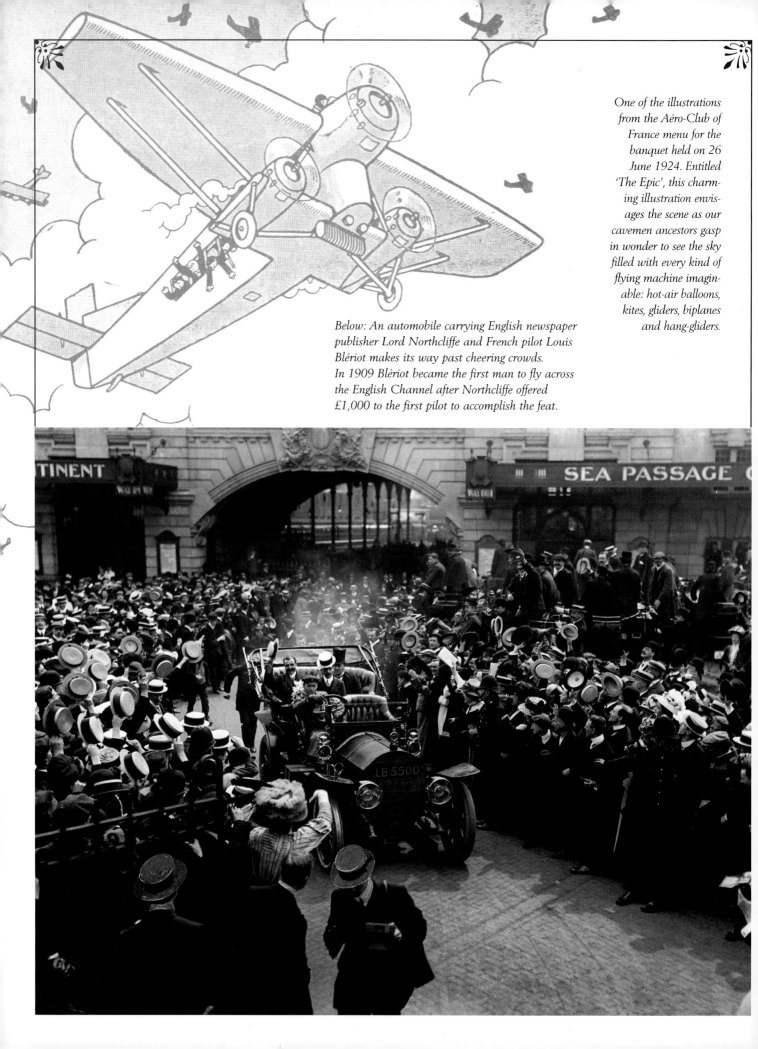

One of the illustrations from the Aéro-Club of France menu for the banquet held on 26 June 1924. Entitled 'The Epic', this charming illustration envisages the scene as our cavemen ancestors gasp in wonder to see the sky filled with every kind of flying machine imaginable: hot-air balloons, kites, gliders, biplanes and hang-gliders.

Below: An automobile carrying English newspaper publisher Lord Northcliffe and French pilot Louis Blériot makes its way past cheering crowds. In 1909 Blériot became the first man to fly across the English Channel after Northcliffe offered £1,000 to the first pilot to accomplish the feat.

L'ÉPOPÉE

THE FOURTH WOMEN'S WORLD GAMES

LONDON

The banquet held in August 1934 was to celebrate the fourth Women's World Games, which were held in London.

These Games marked a very important stage in improving women's sport internationally. The Women's World Games were started by a Frenchwoman, Alice Milliat, in direct response to the repeated refusal of the International Olympic Committee and the International Amateur Athletic Federation to put women's track and field on the programme of the Olympic Games.

Women had competed at the Games since 1900 in tennis, golf, archery, gymnastics, skating and swimming, but not the prestigious 'track and field'. Milliat decided they would have to stage an Olympics of their own. The first Women's Olympic Games was a one-day track meeting in Paris in 1922. Eighteen athletes broke world records before a crowd of 20,000 people. The second Games were held in Gothenberg, Sweden, in 1926 where women from ten nations took part.

The prestige of women's track and field was growing fast and the International Amateur Athletic Federation wanted control of it. They negotiated with Milliat, who agreed to change the name of the event from the Women's Olympics to the Women's World Games, in exchange for ten events at the Olympic Games. Milliat kept her part of the bargain, but the Federation only granted five events.

The final Women's Games were held in London in 1934, after which the International Amateur Athletic Federation took over women's track and field. Alice Milliat deserves to be remembered with honour as the first to push

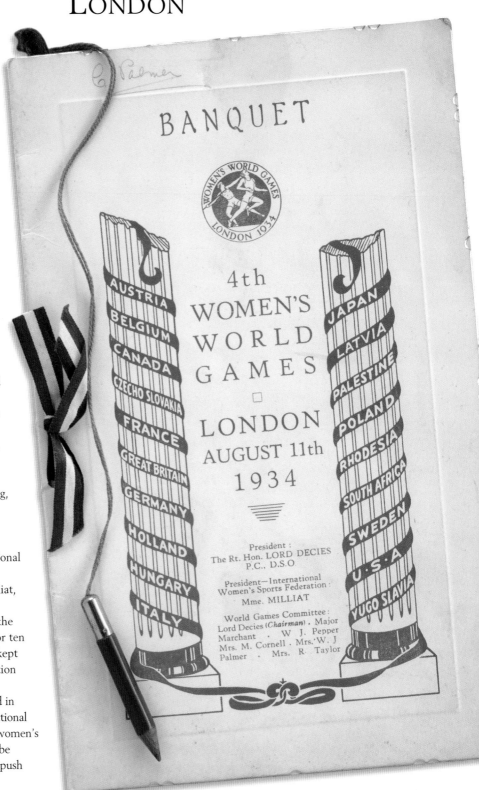

BANQUET

WOMEN'S WORLD GAMES · LONDON 1934

4th WOMEN'S WORLD GAMES

LONDON AUGUST 11th 1934

AUSTRIA · BELGIUM · CANADA · CZECHO SLOVAKIA · FRANCE · GREAT BRITAIN · GERMANY · HOLLAND · HUNGARY · ITALY

JAPAN · LATVIA · PALESTINE · POLAND · RHODESIA · SOUTH AFRICA · SWEDEN · U·S·A · YUGO SLAVIA

President:
The Rt. Hon. LORD DECIES
P.C., D.S.O.

President—International
Women's Sports Federation:
Mme. MILLIAT

World Games Committee:
Lord Decies (Chairman) · Major Marchant · W. J. Pepper · Mrs. M. Cornell · Mrs. W. J. Palmer · Mrs. R. Taylor

MENU

Hors d'œuvres au Choix
Saumon Fume

Oxtail Fleuri au Madere
Creme Lamballe

Filet de Sole Breval
Fleurons

Ris de Veau Financiere
Langue de Boeuf
Petits Pois au Beurre
Pommes Duchesse

Sorbet au Kummel

Poulet Roti 2 Sauces
Salade D'Orange

Poire Praline
Bombe Glace Vanille
Friandises

Croute au Fromage

Cafe

TOASTS

H.M. THE KING
Proposed by THE CHAIRMAN

THE GUESTS
Proposed by THE CHAIRMAN
Reply by MADAME MILLIAT
Dr. TOSAKU KINOSHITA

THE OFFICIALS
Proposed by W. J. PEPPER, Esq.
A.A.A. & World Games Committee
Reply by Mrs. M. CORNELL
Hon Sec W.A.A.A. & World Games Committee
Mrs. R. TAYLOR
World Games Committee

THE WINNING NATION
Proposed by Mrs. C. PALMER
Hon. Treasurer W.A.A.A. & World Games Committee
Reply by a Representative of the Winning Nation

THE CHAIRMAN
Proposed by MAJOR MARCHANT

DANCE MUSIC by THE SILVER ACES
---- under the direction of W. J. LEE ----

MENU

Hors-d'Oeuvres
Smoked Salmon

Oxtail Soup with Madeira
Fresh Pea Soup

Fillet of Sole with Pastry
Shapes

Sweetbreads Garnished
with Cocks' Combs and
Kidneys, Mushrooms,
Olives, Dumplings and
Truffles
Tongue
Peas in Butter
Puréed Potatoes

Sorbet with Liqueur

Roast Chicken with Two
Sauces
Orange Salad

Pears with Crushed
Sugared Almonds
Vanilla Ice Cream Mould
Sweetmeats

Cheese Pastries
Coffee

the International Olympic Committee towards equality for women in sport.

This dinner was held in honour of these final Games. It is a lavish, sumptuous meal, with a sorbet in the middle to cleanse the palate. The sweetbreads dish is the most elaborate, with an amazing garnish of cocks' combs and kidneys, mushrooms, olives, dumplings and truffles. The women were doing themselves proud.

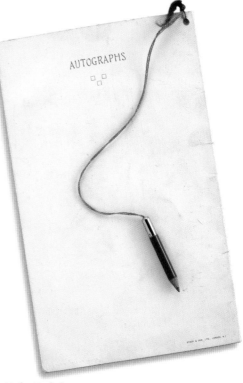

Babe Didrikson wins the 80-Meter Hurdle Race in Los Angeles, 5 August 1932.

THE BRITISH OLYMPIC ASSOCIATION

THE DORCHESTER, LONDON

The annual dinner of the British Olympic Association was held at the Dorchester Hotel on 6 June 1939. A number of the guests were previous medal winners, including the legendary Harold Abrahams, who won the gold medal for the 100 metres in the 1924 Olympics, a feat immortalized in the film *Chariots of Fire*.

Also present was the hero rowing champion Jack Beresford, who won five medals, three gold and two silver, in five consecutive Olympics between 1920 and 1936. He was champion sculler of Great Britain for seven consecutive seasons from 1920, and at Henley Annual Regatta he won the Diamond Sculls four times. Jack was the son of a Polish furniture maker, Julius Beresford, who had also won a silver medal for rowing at the 1912 Games in Helsinki.

The guests at the dinner may not have realized it, but the previous Olympic Games in Berlin, 1936, would be the last to be held before World War II broke out. It would be 1952 before the next Games were held in Helsinki.

The dinner is quite elaborate for the period, and perhaps not entirely suitable for athletes! The most elaborate dish is the fillet of turbot Dugléré. It was named after a pupil of the famous chef Carême who became Chef de Cuisine to the Rothschild family. Turbot is a very large flat fish, and is regarded as a great delicacy. In this recipe the filleted fish is laid on a bed of tomatoes and herbs, sprinkled with butter and wine and baked in the oven. It is served with a white cream sauce.

The salad Suzette, as often happens, was named after someone, but there is no record of who or why. Perhaps it had an orange-flavoured dressing, like the famous crêpe Suzette.

THE BRITISH OLYMPIC ASSOCIATION

ANNUAL DINNER 1939

MENU AND TABLE PLAN

Above and right: Menu and table plan for the annual dinner of the British Olympic Association, held at the Dorchester, London, on 6 June 1939.

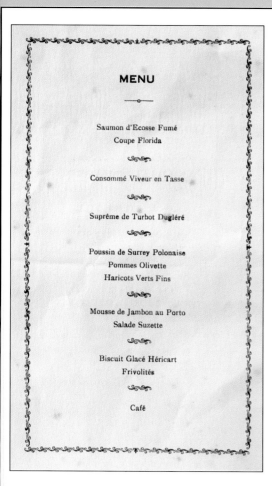

MENU

Saumon d'Ecosse Fumé
Coupe Florida

〜

Consommé Viveur en Tasse

〜

Suprême de Turbot Dugléré

〜

Poussin de Surrey Polonaise
Pommes Olivette
Haricots Verts Fins

〜

Mousse de Jambon au Porto
Salade Suzette

〜

Biscuit Glacé Héricart
Frivolités

Café

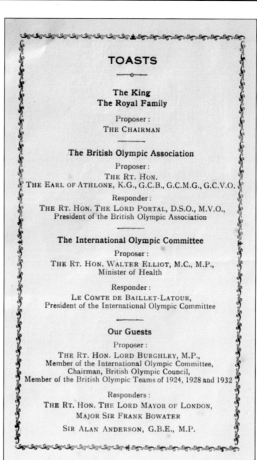

TOASTS

The King
The Royal Family

Proposer:
THE CHAIRMAN

The British Olympic Association

Proposer:
THE RT. HON.
THE EARL OF ATHLONE, K.G., G.C.B., G.C.M.G., G.C.V.O.

Responder:
THE RT. HON. THE LORD PORTAL, D.S.O., M.V.O.,
President of the British Olympic Association

The International Olympic Committee

Proposer:
THE RT. HON. WALTER ELLIOT, M.C., M.P.,
Minister of Health

Responder:
LE COMTE DE BAILLET-LATOUR,
President of the International Olympic Committee

Our Guests

Proposer:
THE RT. HON. LORD BURGHLEY, M.P.,
Member of the International Olympic Committee,
Chairman, British Olympic Council,
Member of the British Olympic Teams of 1924, 1928 and 1932

Responders:
THE RT. HON. THE LORD MAYOR OF LONDON,
MAJOR SIR FRANK BOWATER
SIR ALAN ANDERSON, G.B.E., M.P.

*Left: List of toasts to be
proposed at the British
Olympic Association
Dinner, 1939.*

MENU

Smoked Salmon
Fruit Salad

Clear Soup

Fillet of Turbot, Baked on a Bed
of Tomatoes and Herbs and
Served with a White Sauce

Baby Chicken in a White Sauce
wih Sour Cream, Horseradish,
Fennel and Lemon Juice
Potatoes
Green Beans

Ham Mousse with Port
Salad

Neapolitan Ice Cream
Sweetmeats

Coffee

TOP TABLE

Right Hand Side of Chairman.

— Mr. Douglas Roby.
— Mr. J. G. Merrick, I.O.C., Canada.
— Mr. Ernst Krogius, I.O.C., Finland.
— Baroness Schimmelpenninck van der Oye
— Alderman and Sheriff G. Godfrey Warr.
— Mrs. Godfrey Warr.
— Mr. A. Bolonachi, I.O.C., Greece.
— The Marchioness of Clydesdale.
— Senator Jules de Musza, I.O.C., Hungary.
— The Lady Burghley.
— Sir George Chrystal, K.C.B., President Civil Service Sports Council.
— H.R.H. Princess Axel of Denmark.
— Sir Alan Anderson, G.B.E., M.P.
— Madame A. Bolonachi.
— The Lord Wigram, G.C.B., G.C.V.O., C.S.I.
— The Lady Mayoress.
— Count de Baillet-Latour, President International Olympic Committee.
— The Rt. Hon. The Lord Mayor.
— H.R.H. Princess Alice Countess of Athlone.
— Chairman—THE LORD PORTAL, D.S.O., M.V.O., President British Olympic Association.
— Major-General The Earl of Athlone, K.G., G.C.B., G.C.M.G., G.C.V.O., D.S.O.
— The Lady Portal, M.B.E.
— The Rt. Hon. Walter Elliot, M.C., M.P., Minister of Health.
— The Lord Burghley, M.P., Chairman British Olympic Council, I.O.C., Great Britain.
— Mrs. Edstrom.
— Air Chief Marshal Sir Cyril Newall, G.C.B., C.M.G., C.B.E., President Royal Air Force Sports Board.
— Mr. J. S. Edstrom, I.O.C., Sweden.
— Mrs. Walter Elliot.
— The Marquess of Clydesdale, A.F.C., M.P., Vice-Chairman British Olympic Council.
— Mr. R. Seppala, The Finnish Charge d'Affaires.
— Count Penha-Garcia, I.O.C., Portugal.
— Sir James Leigh-Wood, K.B.E., C.B., C.M.G., Chairman British Empire Games Federation, British Olympic Council.
— Mrs. Krogius.
— Mr. Sheriff Frederick Rowland.
— Mrs. Frederick Rowland.
— Marquis de Polignac, I.O.C., France.
— Countess Bonacossa.
— Professor Dr. F. Bucar, I.O.C., Jugoslavia.
— His Excellency Dr. C. T. Wang, I.O.C., China.

Left Hand Side of Chairman.

Mr. P. J. Mulqueen, President Canadian Olympic Association.
Viscount Newport.
Duke Adolf zu Mecklenburg, I.O.C., Germany.
Lt.-Comdr. Thomas Woodroffe.
Lady Fearnley.
Mr. J. Lee Barrett.
Sir Noel Curtis-Bennett, K.C.V.O., I.O.C., Great Britain.
Mr. Joakim Puhk, I.O.C., Estonia.
Mrs. Lindblom.

— Mr. J. J. Keane, I.O.C., Eire.
— Count Bonacossa, I.O.C., Italy.
— Lt.-Col. J. R. C. Gannon, M.V.O., Official Olympic Games 1936.
— Dr. Karl Ritter von Halt, I.O.C., Germany.
— The Lord Aberdare, I.O.C., Great Britain.
— Mrs. Matuszewski.
— Mr. A. E. Porritt, M.Ch., F.R.C.S., I.O.C., New Zealand.
— Mrs. Puhk.
— Mr. F. Coudert,

Colonel P. W. Scharroo, I.O.C., Holland.
Mr. Janis Dikmanis, I.O.C., Latvia.
Lady Curtis-Bennett.
His Excellency I. Maturzewski, I.O.C., Poland.
His Excellency Stephan G. Tchaprachikov, I.O.C., Bulgaria.
Mrs. A. E. Porritt.
His Excellency Mohamed Taher Pacha, I.O.C., Egypt.
Mr. F. Pietri, I.O.C., France.
Mr. Cyril Gamon, M.V.O.

— Mr. William Northey, Canadian Olympic Committee.
— Baron Schimmelpenninck van der I.O.C., Holland.
— Mr. Charles Graves.
— Sir Thomas Fearnley, K.B.E., I.O.C., Norway.
— Lady Aberdare.
— H.R.H. Prince Axel of Denmark I.O.C., Denmark.
— Mrs. Pietri.
— Mr. Avery Brundage, I.O.C., United States of America
— Mr. N. de Horthy, I.O.C., Hungary.

THE BRITISH AUTOMOBILE RACING CLUB

GROSVENOR HOUSE HOTEL, LONDON

In November 1967 the annual dinner of the British Automobile Racing Club was held at the Grosvenor House Hotel, London. The menu is notable for its mention of so many famous drivers.

It is signed on the front cover by the World Champion racing driver Graham Hill (father of Damon Hill) and also by racing driver Innes Irland. Graham Hill captured the public's imagination like no other racing driver of the time. He started his career from nothing and showed unbelievable courage, not to mention an appetite for hard work, to reach the very top of his profession. He began racing regularly in 1956 in Lotus and Cooper sports cars. Lotus entered Grand Prix racing in 1958, with Hill as driver, making his debut at Monaco where a wheel fell off. His two seasons with the Lotus 16 were largely unsuccessful, the cars suffering all sorts of failures. In 1960, the year that his son Damon Hill was born, he joined BRM who had won a Grand Prix and were a better bet for improving his career. After a bad year in 1961 when the British four-cylinder cars were outclassed by Ferrari, it was win or bust for the BRM team who were threatened with closure if success was not achieved in 1962. With the new V8-engined car Graham responded brilliantly by winning the Dutch GP and then, after losing seemingly certain triumphs in both the Monaco and the French GP, he took the BRM to three more victories to claim a thoroughly deserved first World Championship. Hill moved to Lotus in 1967, joining Jim Clark, to race the new Lotus 49.

At this dinner various trophies were presented: the Fred W. Dixon Trophy and the BARC Saloon Car Championship Trophy to the 1967 winners, followed by presentation of gold medals to another two outstanding racing drivers, Denis Hulme and Jack Brabham.

Menu

Le Consommé Madrilène

*

Le Suprême de Flétan Nantua

*

Le Carré d'Agneau Richelieu
Les Petits Pois au Beurre
Les Pommes Olivettes

*

L'Ananas Voilé en Surprise à l'Orientale
Le Parfait Glacé Vanille

*

Le Café

MENU

Clear Soup with Tomato Juice

Fillet of Halibut in a Crayfish
and Truffle Sauce

Loin of Lamb, Garnished wih
Stuffed Tomatoes and
Mushrooms, Braised Lettuce
and Roast Potatoes
Peas in Butter
Potatoes

Pineapple, Filled with Fresh
Fruit and Almonds in Kirsch
Vanilla-Flavoured Ice Cream
Mould

Coffee

Toasts and Presentations

THE QUEEN

❖

An Address of Welcome to the Assembled Company
Members and Guests
by
LEONARD F. DYER
Vice-President of the Club

❖

Introduction by
W. W. PAUL
Chairman of the Council
to the presentation of the
FRED. W. DIXON CHALLENGE TROPHY
and
B. A.R.C. SALOON CAR CHAMPIONSHIP TROPHY
to the 1967 winners
followed by
the Presentation of the Trophies
by
LEONARD F. DYER

❖

Presentation to
LEONARD F. DYER
by
W. W. PAUL
Chairman of the Council

❖

PRESENTATION OF GOLD MEDALS
to
DENIS HULME and JACK BRABHAM, O.B.E.

TRUMPETERS OF THE COLDSTREAM GUARDS
By kind permission of Colonel Sir Ian Jardine, Bart., O.B.E., M.C.,
Commanding Coldstream Guards
Director of Music—Captain Trevor L. Sharpe, M.B.E., L.R.A.M.,
A.R.C.M., p.s.m. Coldstream Guards

Denis Hulme was a New Zealander, known as 'The Bear' because of his stocky physique and build. He liked to drive barefoot, so when he took up racing the newspapers called him 'the barefoot boy from te Puke'. In 1960 he won the New Zealand International Grand Prix Association's Driver-to-Europe award, a scholarship which had also boosted the careers of Bruce McLaren and Chris Amon. In 1965 Jack Brabham invited him to join his Formula One team, and after Black Jack took his third World Championship in 1966, Hulme earned the title in 1967.

Jack Brabham, an Australian, had won the world title in 1966 in the BT19, a car he had built himself (itself a first). He then won the Formula One Constructions Championship in 1966 and 1967. He was made an OBE in 1967, the first driver in history to be knighted for his services to motor sport.

In Edwardian times sportsmen (mostly involved in shooting, fishing and racing) ate gargantuan quantities. This is a short menu by comparison, but honour is done, with superb dishes such as halibut in a crayfish and truffle sauce, loin of lamb, and a hollowed-out pineapple filled with fresh fruit and almonds steeped in kirsch.

British Formula One racing car driver Graham Hill of Team Lotus competes in the 1967 Watkins Glen Formula One Grand Prix.

Potage à la Tortue, Consommé Claire, Crême de Riz à la PolonaiseTête
Saumon Mayonnaise, Truite Saumonée Froide, Cailles à la Bordeaux
à l'Archiduc, Les Poulets Gras au Cresson, Langue de Boeuf Fumée,
Parfait de Foie Gras, Les Epinards aux Croûtons, Jambon de Bayo
d'Oranges, Petits Savarins au Kirsch, Meringues à la Chantilly, Bûche
de Veau en Tortue, Petite Marmite, Salade de Homard, Barquettes d'E
Salmis de Gelinottes, Riz de Veau, Filets de Sole Mornay, Canetons
Suprême de Volaille aux Truffes, Turbot Sauce Hollandaise, Oeufs de G
Haricots Verts, Filet de Boeuf, Chapon du Mans, Bombe Glacée, Gelée
Potage à la Tortue, Consommé Claire, Crême de Riz à la PolonaiseTête
Saumon Mayonnaise, Truite Saumonée Froide, Cailles à la Bordeaux
à l'Archiduc, Les Poulets Gras au Cresson, Langue de Boeuf Fumée,
Parfait de Foie Gras, Les Epinards aux Croûtons, Jambon de Bayo
d'Oranges, Petits Savarins au Kirsch, Meringues à la Chantilly, Bûche
de Veau en Tortue, Petite Marmite, Salade de Homard, Barquettes d'E
Salmis de Gelinottes, Riz de Veau, Filets de Sole Mornay, Canetons
Suprême de Volaille aux Truffes, Turbot Sauce Hollandaise, Oeufs de G
Haricots Verts, Filet de Boeuf, Chapon du Mans, Bombe Glacée, Gelée
Potage à la Tortue, Consommé Claire, Crême de Riz à la PolonaiseTête
Saumon Mayonnaise, Truite Saumonée Froide, Cailles à la Bordeaux
à l'Archiduc, Les Poulets Gras au Cresson, Langue de Boeuf Fumée,
Parfait de Foie Gras, Les Epinards aux Croûtons, Jambon de Bayo
d'Oranges, Petits Savarins au Kirsch, Meringues à la Chantilly, Bûche
de Veau en Tortue, Petite Marmite, Salade de Homard, Barquettes d'E
Salmis de Gelinottes, Riz de Veau, Filets de Sole Mornay, Canetons
Suprême de Volaille aux Truffes, Turbot Sauce Hollandaise, Oeufs de G
Haricots Verts, Filet de Boeuf, Chapon du Mans, Bombe Glacée, Gelée

Special Festivities

Special occasions give illustrators a wonderful opportunity to express their

talents, as can be seen with these charming menus for Christmas, Boxing Day

and festivals such as Thanksgiving and St Patrick's Day. Art Deco style is used

for four delightful menus for Boxing Day at the Royal Bath Hotel in 1936.

Another striking Art Deco menu is for Christmas Day at the Hotel Cecil, 1923,

where a winter scene with a jolly girl throwing a snowball sums up the festive

mood. A Thanksgiving menu from Schofield Barracks in Hawaii, showing the US

flags and eagle, with a magnificent plump turkey, is typical of the late 1930s.

Burns Night, Scotland's tribute to its famous poet, also gives the artist plenty of

scope, with shields, claymores, sporrans and tartan decorating the menu for a

Glasgow Burns Supper for 1921. By contrast the St Patrick's Day menu for 1895

is much more delicate, with a border of shamrock and harps in pale green.

❧ 1895 ❧

ST PATRICK'S DAY CONVIVIALITY

CAFÉ ROYAL, LONDON

The Friendly Brothers of St Patrick held a dinner at the Café Royal, London, in 1895 to celebrate the feast of St Patrick, Ireland's patron saint. St Patrick's Day is traditionally celebrated on 17 March but celebrations go on all week in a friendly Irish atmosphere, with traditional music, excellent food and Guinness stout.

Guinness was first produced in Dublin in 1759 by Arthur Guinness, who was a leading figure in the Friendly Brothers of St Patrick. This charitable organization was formed over 240 years ago and continues to grow, as the celebration of St Patrick becomes an ever more global event.

This was a rich, heavy dinner, typical of the period, and no doubt was washed down with fine wines as well as Guinness.

An extract from *The Royal Gazette* (New York), 18 March 1780:
The Anniversary of Saint Patrick was yesterday celebrated with the wonted conviviality. In the morning a most elegant breakfast and ball were given at Mr. Hick's by the Members of the amiable Society of Friendly Brothers of St. Patrick to all the Officers of the Army and Navy and the Gentlemen of the City. In the afternoon many entertainments were likewise given, and the night closed with all the real jocundity which ever distinguished that brave & generous nation, Great Britain's beloved Sister. Yesterday, (in honour of the Anniversary of St. Patrick, tutelar Saint of that Kingdom) the regiment of Volunteers of Ireland, quartered on Jamaica, (Long-Island) were munificently entertained by their Colonel, the Right Honourable Lord Rawdon.

A SONG,
Sung Yesterday at Jamaica before the Volunteers of
  Ireland, it being St. Patrick's Day.
  By Barny Thomson,, Piper to that Regiment.
  Tune— "Langolee"
Success to the shamrogue, and all those who wear it,
Be honour their portion wherever they go,
May riches attend them, and store of good claret,
For how to employ them sure none better know;
Every foe surveys them with terror,
But every silk petticoat wishes them nearer,
So Yankee keep off, or you'll soon learn your error,
For Paddy shall prostrate lay ev'ry foe.
This day, (but the year I can't rightly determine)
St. Patrick the vipers did chase from this land,
Let's see if like him we can't sweep off the vermin
Who dare 'gainst the sons of the shamrogue to stand;
Hand in hand! let's carrol this chorus,
"As long as the blessings of Ireland hang o'er us,
"The crest of rebellion shall tremble before us,
"Like brothers while thus we march hand in hand!"
St. George & St. Patrick, St. Andrew, St. David,
Together may laugh at all Europe in arms,
Fair conquest her standard has o'er their heads waved
And glory has on them conferr'd all her charms!
War's alarms! to us are a pleasure,
Since honour our danger repays in full measure,
And all those who join us shall find we have leisure,
To think of our sport ev'n in war's alarms!

MENU

Hors d'oeuvres

Beef Broth
Cream of Artichoke Soup

Turbot with Cheese Sauce
Fillet of Sole in Brown Fish Sauce with
Butter and Herbs

Spiced Veal Garnished with Fresh
Vegetables

Chicken Breast with Truffles
Saddle of Welsh Lamb with

Gooseberry Jelly

Baby Potatoes Sautéed in Butter
Green Beans

York Ham with Champagne Sauce

Asparagus with Cream Sauce

Iced Fruit Pudding
Cheese
Dessert

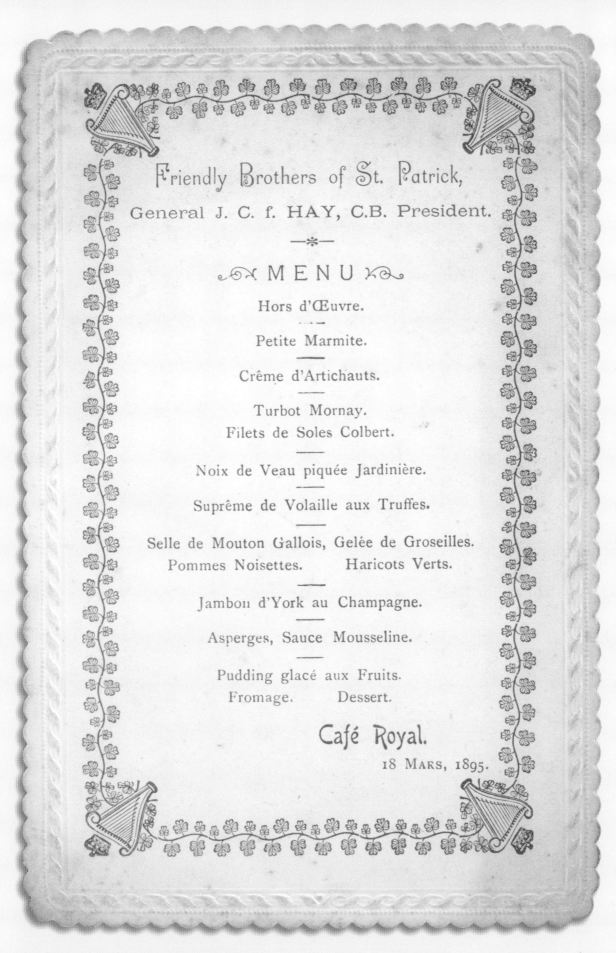

Friendly Brothers of St. Patrick,
General J. C. f. HAY, C.B. President.

—*—

MENU

Hors d'Œuvre.

———

Petite Marmite.

———

Crême d'Artichauts.

———

Turbot Mornay.
Filets de Soles Colbert.

———

Noix de Veau piquée Jardinière.

———

Suprême de Volaille aux Truffes.

———

Selle de Mouton Gallois, Gelée de Groseilles.
Pommes Noisettes.   Haricots Verts.

———

Jambon d'York au Champagne.

———

Asperges, Sauce Mousseline.

———

Pudding glacé aux Fruits.
Fromage.   Dessert.

Café Royal.

18 Mars, 1895.

Menu for the St Patrick's Day dinner held at the
Café Royal, London, 18 March 1895.

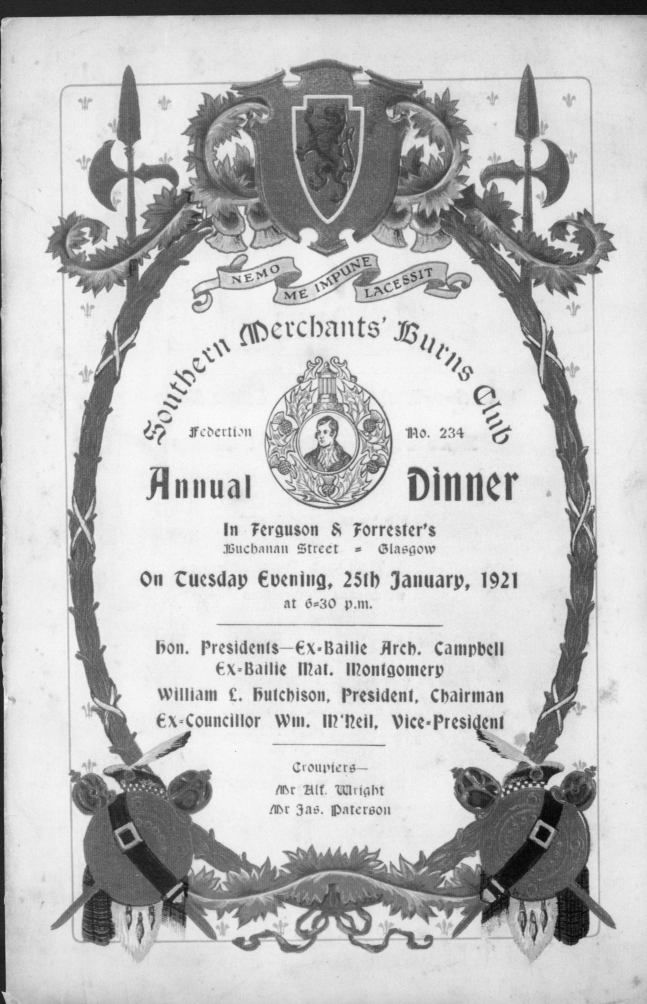

NEMO ME IMPUNE LACESSIT

Southern Merchants' Burns Club

Federtion   No. 234

Annual   **Dinner**

In Ferguson & Forrester's
Buchanan Street = Glasgow

On Tuesday Evening, 25th January, 1921
at 6=30 p.m.

Hon. Presidents—Ex=Bailie Arch. Campbell
Ex=Bailie Mat. Montgomery

William L. Hutchison, President, Chairman

Ex=Councillor Wm. M'Neil, Vice=President

Croupiers—
Mr Alf. Wright
Mr Jas. Paterson

BURNS NIGHT CELEBRATION

FERGUSON AND FORRESTER'S, GLASGOW

T his menu is for a Burns Night dinner on 25 January 1921, held in Ferguson and Forrester's at Buchanan Street, Glasgow. It is beautifully illustrated with swords and shields. Burns suppers have been part of the Scottish culture for over 200 years as a means of commemorating their best-loved poet. And when Burns immortalized haggis in verse he created a link that is maintained to this day. Close friends of Burns started the ritual a few years after his death in 1796 as a tribute to his memory, and the basic format for the evening has remained unchanged since that time.

The company are asked to stand to receive the haggis. A piper then leads the chef carrying the haggis to the top table, while the guests accompany them with a slow handclap. The invited guest then recites Burns' famous poem *To a Haggis*. When he reaches the line 'an cut you up wi' ready slight', he cuts open the haggis with a sharp knife. It is customary for the company to applaud the speaker, then stand again and toast the haggis with a glass of whisky.

Haggis is really just a rather unusual sausage. It is cooked in a sheep's stomach bag, and consists of the heart, liver and lungs of a sheep, chopped onion, pinhead oatmeal, shredded beef suet, salt, pepper and other flavourings to taste. Sometimes nutmeg, cayenne pepper

Toast and Harmony

THE KING, QUEEN AND ROYAL FAMILY

National Anthem ... ... THE CHAIRMAN

Reading—"Address to a Haggis" ... ... THE COMPANY

The Immortal Memory—Rev. R. Montgomerie Hardie, ... Mr C. W. ANDERSON
B.D. ("Cockpen")

"Honoured more and more as the years roll by"

Song—" There was a lad was born in Kyle" ... Mr D. M. GILCHRIST

Toast - Magistrates and Town Council" Parish Councillor ALEX. MARTIN

Song—"O' a' the airts" ... ...

Reply ... ... Mr HUGH M'GILL

Reading—" Death and Dr. Hornbook" ... Bailie JAMES A. STEWART

Toast—Southern Merchants' Burns Club ... Mr W. WEIR

"Oor Ain Club" ... Mr DONALD M'KAY KERR

Song—(Scotch Humorous) ...

Reply ... ... Mr W. M'CORMACK

Reading—"Address to the Deil" ... Ex-Bailie ARCH. CAMPBELL

Toast—Guests and Kindred Clubs " ... Mr C. W. ANDERSON

Song—" Ae Fond Kiss" ... Ex-Bailie MAT. MONTGOMERY

Toast—The Chairman ... ... Mr HUGH M'GILL

Song—(Scotch Humorous) ... Ex-Councillor WILLIAM M'NEIL

Reply ... ... Mr W. M'CORMACK

Song—" Scots, Wha Hae " ... ... THE PRESIDENT

... THE COMPANY (P.T.O.)

Pianist = Mr Donald Millar | Piper = Mr Thomas Musgrove

Hon. Secretary = Mr Daniel M'Gregor
5 Barrland Street, Pollokshields

Menu

Cock-a-Leekie   Tattie Soup
—
Biled Cod   Champit Tatties
—
Haggis
and "a wee drappie o't"
—
Roasted Hen
wi' Greens o' some kind
—
Roly Poly   Aipple Tairts
—
Kibbuck on Toast
—
Aipples an' Oranges
—
Coffee

and other spices are added. The bag is sewn up very securely and then boiled for three hours. Haggis is usually served with bashed neeps (mashed swede) and champit tatties (mashed potatoes).

A traditional Burns Night supper always begins with cock-a-leekie soup (chicken and leek soup). On this occasion they omitted the bashed neeps and served boiled cod after the soup (nowadays it might be smoked salmon). The haggis is always served with whisky, though wine might be drunk with the rest of the meal. Roly poly is a steamed suet pudding with jam, and kibbuck is an old name for cheese.

Far left: Colourful menu cover for this Burns Club dinner in Glasgow, 25 January 1921, featuring swords, shields, kilts with sporrans, feathered caps and claymores.

1923
CHRISTMAS DAY DINNER AND DANCING
HOTEL CECIL, LONDON

The Christmas dinner for 1923 at the Hotel Cecil is notable for having dancing as well as a concert to entertain the diners. During the 1920s all-night dancing clubs sprang up in London and New York, although all drinking was illegal in New York – the famous Prohibition.

The Charleston was the dance of the moment and tea dances were held at the best hotels. Night life in London at this time was at its most vibrant, the pavements thronged with theatre-goers and diners. The sparkling lights of the restaurants and hotels gave the streets a brilliance that they did not possess during the day, and the restaurants and dining-rooms of the hotels had an atmosphere of luxury and splendour, soft lights shining on the white tablecloths and brilliant silver, while the strains of the orchestra mingled with the voices and merry laughter.

The menu for this Christmas dinner is signed by the Chef de Cuisine, J. Loustalot. It is full of little jokes and references, such as Santa Claus sole, Cinderella's foie gras, and will-o'-the-wisp plum pudding. Will-o'-the-wisp, also known as Jack o' lantern, is actually a phosphorescence sometimes seen over marshy ground at night: a reference to the tradition of flaming the Christmas pudding in brandy just before it is served. This is a very grand Christmas dinner, featuring turkey stuffed with fresh truffles (incredibly expensive now) and foie gras in aspic. *Bûche de Noël* is the log cake traditionally served in France at Christmas. It is made in the shape of a log and covered with chocolate strips or chocolate butter cream.

MENU

Oysters
Clear Soup
Cream Soup, with Game Purée, Diced Mushrooms in Butter and Madeira

Fillet of Sole

Fillets of Lamb
Artichoke Hearts
Potatoes

Young Turkey Stuffed with Fresh Truffles
Chestnut Cream

Foie Gras in Aspic
Salad

Plum Pudding
Mince Pie

Christmas Log Cake
Sweetmeats

Dessert

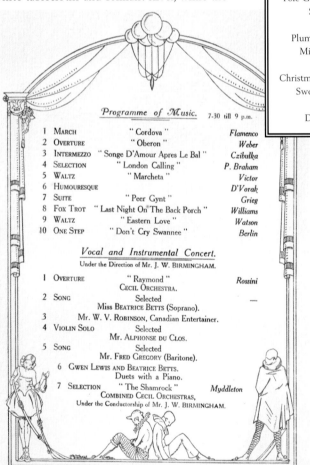

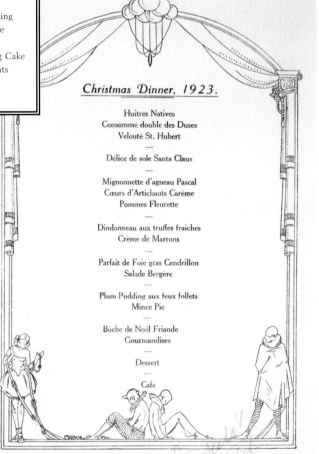

Christmas Greeting

HOTEL CECIL

The attractive cover, in very 1920s style, for the Christmas dinner of 1923 at the Hotel Cecil in London.

GRAND DINING ON BOXING DAY
THE ROYAL BATH HOTEL

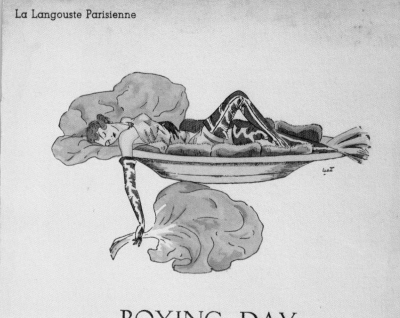

La Langouste Parisienne

BOXING DAY

DECEMBER 26TH :: 1936

ROYAL BATH HOTEL,
BOURNEMOUTH.

For the menu for Boxing Day, 26 December 1936, the hotel commissioned the Parisian artist Lyett to illustrate these different covers. They are a fine example of the Art Deco style.

Opened in 1878, the Royal Bath Hotel attracted the aristocracy and other celebrities, including Prince Henry of Battenburg, Edward VII (when still Prince of Wales), the Empress Eugenie of France, Queen Wilhemina of the Netherlands, Oscar Wilde, Sir Henry Irving, Prime Ministers Disraeli, Gladstone, Asquith and Lloyd George. More recent visitors include the author H. G. Wells and the actor Richard Harris. The grounds of the hotel were used for location shots for the 1977 film *Valentino*, starring the Russian ballet dancer Rudolf Nureyev.

Boxing Day takes its name from the custom of allowing servants to take leave on the day after Christmas. Some employers gave each servant a box containing gifts and bonuses.

As befits such a smart hotel, this is a very elegant and sumptuous menu. It begins with the prized Marenne oysters, noted for their green colour, which comes from the algae in the pools where they are embedded. The '*Perles du Périgord*' refers to the black truffles for which the Périgord region of France is noted. As usual, some dishes are specially named in honour of the occasion, such as chicken breast Bethlehem and salad Nazareth. There is also the patriotic mention of a member of the royal family with Peaches Margaret Rose, in honour of Princess Margaret.

The four Boxing Day menu covers produced by the Royal Bath Hotel in 1936. They were specially commissioned from the Parisian artist Lyett.

MENU

Marenne Oysters	Potatoes with Almonds
Spanish Melon	
	Pastries Filled with Truffles
Profiteroles with Oriental	Salad
Cream	
	Peaches
Spiced Salmon	Sweetmeats
Chicken Breast	Roast Chestnuts
French Sugared Peas	Basket of Fruit

La Perdrix aux Choux

BOXING DAY
December 26th :: 1936

ROYAL BATH HOTEL,
BOURNEMOUTH.

Les Cailles rôties sur Canapé

BOXING DAY
December 26th :: 1936

ROYAL BATH HOTEL,
BOURNEMOUTH.

DINNER.

Les Marennes
Melon d'Alicante

—

La Coupe Yvette aux Profiterolles
Creme Orientale

—

Le Saumon de la Baltique Viveur

—

Le Suprême de Volaille Bethlehem
Petits Pois au Sucre
Pommes Amandine

—

Les Delices d'Alsace
Aux Perles du Périgord
Salade Nazareth

—

Les Pêches Margaret Rose
Mignardises

—

Marrons Grillés

—

Corbeille de Fruits Britannia

La Coupe Jacques

BOXING DAY
December 26th :: 1936

ROYAL BATH HOTEL,
BOURNEMOUTH.

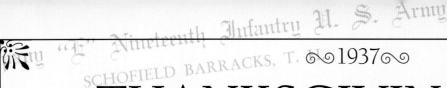

1937
THANKSGIVING WITH THE US ARMY
SCHOFIELD BARRACKS, HAWAII

Whether stationed at home or abroad, the men of the US army can hope for some recognition of the Thanksgiving holiday. But few would expect such a lavish menu as this one for Thanksgiving Dinner at Schofield Barracks, Hawaii, in 1937.

Schofield Barracks were established in 1908 to provide a base for the Army's mobile defence of Pearl Harbor and the whole island of Hawaii. By 1937 the troops there were largely occupied in the maintenance and repair of aircraft and other military vehicles. At this time Hawaii was known as the Territory of Hawaii, as indicated by the abbreviation 'T. H.' on the front of the menu – the island did not become the 50th State of the USA until 1959, and was not the popular vacation destination that it is today. Just four years after this dinner was served, Japanese planes flew over the barracks on their way to bomb Wheeler Field and Pearl Harbor.

This is certainly a generous menu for the troops on Thanksgiving. Not every soldier in the US Army could expect oyster stew as a starter for their dinner, or a choice of six desserts. But as the recipe below, taken from the US Army's *Manual of Mess Management 1941* shows, every soldier could expect their turkey to be roasted with military precision.

Thanksgiving Dinner November 25, 1937

Menu

Oyster Stew	Soda Crackers

Ripe Olives   Stuffed Olives   Sweet Pickles   Celery Hearts

Roast Turkey

Sliced Cold Ham

Oyster Dressing	Cranberry Sauce
Giblet Gravy	Snowflake Potatoes
Candied Sweet Potatoes	Buttered Peas
Creamed Corn	Buttered Asparagus Tips

Chicken Salad

Mince Pie	Pineapple Cream Pie

Fruit Cake   Cocoanut Cake   Devils Food Cake

Bananas   Pears   Apples   Grapes   Plums

Ice Cream

Cigars	Cigarettes

Mixed Drinks

Coffee	Sugar	Cream

TURKEY DINNER FOR AN ARMY

Ingredients: 70 pounds turkey, undrawn or 50 pounds dressed and drawn; 4 pounds onions, minced, browned; 2 pounds fat, butter preferred; 15 pounds bread crumbs; 2 pounds flour

Singe, then clean the turkey well, saving heart, liver, and gizzard, which should be cooked and then minced for use in gravy or dressing. To make the dressing, moisten the bread crumbs with water, mix with onions and giblets, and season with pepper and salt, sage, thyme, or other spices. The bread may be soaked in oyster liquor and oysters added to the dressing. Celery, currants, or raisins may be used instead of onions.

Lemon juice or nuts may be added. Stuff the turkey well with dressing. Sew up with strong thread and tie wings down to the body. Make a batter with the flour and fat, season with salt and pepper and rub the turkey with it before placing in oven. Roast in a slow oven (200–250°F). After the turkey has been in the oven about 20 minutes, add a little hot water and baste every 15 minutes until done. This generally requires about 2½ hours, depending upon the quality of the fowl. Last few minutes of cooking should be at high heat to brown the outside of the turkey. Carve and serve hot with gravy.

Thanksgiving Dinner November 25, 1937

Company "E" Nineteenth Infantry U. S. Army
SCHOFIELD BARRACKS, T. H.

Left: Colourful menu cover for the Thanksgiving Dinner at Schofield Barracks.

COCOANUT TREE

Thanksgiving Dinner November 25, 1937

Menu

Oyster Stew   Soda Crackers

Ripe Olives   Stuffed Olives   Sweet Pickles   Celery Hearts

Roast Turkey

Sliced Cold Ham

Oyster Dressing   Cranberry Sauce

Giblet Gravy   Snowflake Potatoes

Candied Sweet Potatoes   Buttered Peas

Creamed Corn   Buttered Asparagus Tips

Chicken Salad

Mince Pie   Pineapple Cream Pie

Fruit Cake   Cocoanut Cake   Devils Food Cake

Bananas   Pears   Apples   Grapes   Plums

Ice Cream

Cigars   Cigarettes

Mixed Drinks

Coffee   Sugar   Cream

Saumon Mayonnaise, Truite Saumonée Froide, Cailles à la Bordeaux à l'Archiduc, Les Poulets Gras au Cresson, Langue de Boeuf Fumée, Parfait de Foie Gras, Les Epinards aux Croûtons, Jambon de Bayon d'Oranges, Petits Savarins au Kirsch, Meringues à la Chantilly, Bûche de Veau en Tortue, Petite Marmite, Salade de Homard, Barquettes d'E Salmis de Gelinottes, Riz de Veau, Filets de Sole Mornay, Canetons Suprême de Volaille aux Truffes, Turbot Sauce Hollandaise, Oeufs de P Haricots Verts, Filet de Boeuf, Chapon du Mans, Bombe Glacée, Ge Noël, Potage à la Tortue, Consommé Claire, Crême de Riz à la Polon d'Ecrevisses, Saumon Mayonnaise, Truite Saumonée Froide, Cailles à Canetons de Rouen à l'Archiduc, Les Poulets Gras au Cresson, Langue Oeufs de Pluviers, Parfait de Foie Gras, Les Epinards aux Croûtons, J Glacée, Gelée d'Oranges, Petits Savarins au Kirsch, Meringues à la C la PolonaiseTête de Veau en Tortue, Petite Marmite, Salade de Hon Cailles à la Bordeaux, Salmis de Gelinottes, Riz de Veau, Filets de Sole de Boeuf Fumée, Suprême de Volaille aux Truffes, Turbot Sauce Ho Jambon de Bayonne, Haricots Verts, Filet de Boeuf, Chapon du Ma Chantilly, Bûche de Noël, Potage à la Tortue, Consommé Claire, Crê Homard, Barquettes d'Ecrevisses, Saumon Mayonnaise, Truite Saumo Sole Mornay, Canetons de Rouen à l'Archiduc, Les Poulets Gras au C Hollandaise, Oeufs de Pluviers, Parfait de Foie Gras, Les Epinards au Mans, Bombe Glacée, Gelée d'Oranges, Petits Savarins au Kirsch, M Crême de Riz à la PolonaiseTête de Veau en Tortue, Petite Marmit Saumonée Froide, Cailles à la Bordeaux, Salmis de Gelinottes, Riz de au Cresson, Langue de Boeuf Fumée, Suprême de Volaille aux Truffes, aux Croûtons, Jambon de Bayonne, Haricots Verts, Filet de Boeuf, Meringues à la Chantilly, Bûche de Noël, Suprême de Volaille aux

Dining in Style

The heyday of the grand hotels and restaurants was from the late 1880s up to the beginning of World War II; from the introduction of elevators, electric lights and hot running water to en-suite bathrooms in every bedroom. Kings, queens, business tycoons and movie stars stayed at the most prestigious hotels. In London, royalty and statesmen favoured Claridge's, and movie stars the Savoy, while in New York the Waldorf was a particular favourite of the élite. These were magnificent, imposing buildings, vying with each other in luxurious surroundings: public rooms decorated with murals, marble pillars and ornate plaster mouldings, with a sweeping staircase to make the perfect entrance. One innovation was hand-painted tiles, introduced to great success at the Criterion in Piccadilly, London, which could afford the best in splendid decoration. The early 20th century saw the introduction of Art Deco and Art Nouveau styles, some of which can still be seen, in Claridge's, for example.

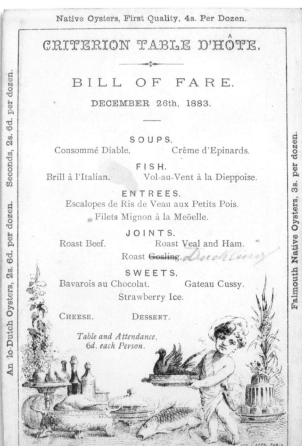

SERVED WITH STYLE

CRITERION RESTAURANT, LONDON

This menu from the Criterion Restaurant on Boxing Day, 26 December 1883, is a fine example of the lithographers' art, signed by Appel of Paris. It was not uncommon for the top restaurants to commission artists to illustrate their menus. The artist has shown his sense of humour in the scene where the hare, in the guise of the chef, threatens the hunter with a knife. The Criterion contained luncheon and dining rooms, a theatre and a music hall, all decorated in sumptuous neo-Byzantine style. The building has recently been restored and revamped and is now open again as a gourmet restaurant.

The menu is the typical lavish fare of the time, with two kinds of soup, fish and entrée dishes as well as roast joints and sweets. We don't know what Gâteau Cussy was. Various dishes have been named after Cussy, who was Prefect of the Palace under Napoleon I, and a famous gourmet.

Above and right: The humorous illustrations for the Criterion menu were specially commissioned from a French lithographer.

MENU

Clear Soup, Garnished with Small Rounds of Toasted Cheese and Cayenne	Veal Sweetbreads with Peas Fillet of Beef Roast Beef, Roast Veal and Ham, Roast Duckling
Cream of Spinach Soup	
Brill with Mushrooms Vol-au-Vents Filled with Shellfish and Crayfish Tails in White Wine Sauce	Chocolate Cream Mould Gâteau Strawberry Ice Cheese Dessert

THE CRITERION

Piccadilly - Circus. LONDON.

THE CRITERION

Piccadilly - Circus. LONDON.

THE CRITERION

Piccadilly - Circus. LONDON.

THE CRITERION

Piccadilly - Circus. LONDON.

ELEGANCE AND LUXURY
THE PALACE HOTEL, SAN FRANCISCO

This is the dinner menu for 1 July 1891, at the Palace Hotel, San Francisco.

The Palace Hotel was the inspiration of William Ralston, President of the Bank of California. He wanted to create a hotel of elegance and luxury to rival the European hotels of the day, commissioning an architect to design a magnificent hotel. He achieved his goal, but the hotel cost a staggering five million dollars. Just weeks before the Palace's grand opening, he was told the Bank of California would close. The next day, Ralston's body was found floating in San Francisco Bay. His partner, Senator William Sharon, was undeterred and opened the hotel on 2 October 1875 to great acclaim.

Even famous guests stood in awe of its magnificence. They were fascinated by the hotel's four hydraulic elevators, known as 'rising rooms'. Each room was equipped with an electronic call button, so that guests could fulfil their every requirement.

In 1906 a massive earthquake shook San Francisco. The Palace Hotel survived the earthquake, but was badly damaged by the fires that engulfed the city. Following the earthquake, the hotel closed for restoration to its former glory. The Garden Court Restaurant, with its incredible architecture, domed stained-glass ceiling and Austrian crystal chandeliers, became the site for some of the nation's most prestigious events.

The menu is lavish, but unlike European menus of the time it is in English, with the odd French word or phrase. The braised beef *Milanaise* is garnished with macaroni cheese, ham, tongue, mushrooms and truffles in tomato sauce. Leg of mutton *à l'Anglaise* is boiled mutton cooked with carrots and onions, and served with a caper sauce. Potatoes *Parisienne* are tiny potatoes cooked in butter then tossed in melted meat jelly or stock. The lamb sweetbreads *parisiens* has a garnish of artichoke hearts. In the desserts, *mille-feuilles* are layers of flaky pastry, sandwiched with rum-flavoured cream, while *palmiers* are puff-pastry shapes.

Dinner.
Wednesday, July 1, 1891.

MENU

Soup	Germiny	Beef Broth

Boiled Salmon, Shrimp Sauce

Fish   Fresh Anchovies

Potatoes Parisienne

Boiled   Corned Beef and Cabbage

Leg of Mutton à l'Anglaise

Entrees
Beef Braisé, à la Milanaise
Caisse of Lamb Sweetbreads à la Parisienne
Fried Calf's Brains, Tomato Sauce

Cold
Lamb   Veal
Ham   Beef Tongue
Roast Beef   Celery Salad

Roast
Beef   Veal
Spring Lamb, Mint Sauce
Goose

Vegetables
Rice   Beets   Stewed Tomatoes
Mashed Potatoes   Baked Potatoes
Green Peas   Cauliflower

Dessert
Scotch Pudding, Rhum Sauce   Strawberry Tartelette
Peach Pie   Mille Feuille au Rhum
Lemon Sponge Cake   Palmiers au Sucre

Ice Cream
Banana Ice Cream   Raspberry Water Ice

Almonds   English Walnuts   Raisins
Fruit   COFFEE   Cheese

DINNER, 6 to 8 P. M.
Late Supper Served in Restaurant, from 8 to 11:30 P. M.

PLEASE REPORT ANY INATTENTION OR DELAY TO THE STEWARD.

AMUSEMENTS
ALCAZAR THEATRE—Frederic Bryton, in The Streets of New York.
Performance every Evening and Saturday Matinee.

Palace Hotel Wines.

PURE CALIFORNIA WINES, DIRECT FROM VINEYARD.

	Pts.	Qts.		Pts.	Qts.
Eclipse Ext. Dry (Champagne)..	$1 25	$2 50	Livermore Wines, Haut Sauterne, $	50	$1 00
NAPA VALLEY WINES			" " Malbec......	40	75
Zinfandel......................	30	50	" " Riesling......	40	75
Riesling........................	30	50	" " Burgundy....	40	75
Private Stock Claret..........	50	1 00	**WETMORE'S CRESTA BLANCA VINTAGE.**		
Private Stock Hock...........	50	1 00	**Gold Medal Paris Exposition 1889.**		
Vine Cliff Claret..............	1 00	2 00	Sauterne, Souvenier...........	75	1 25
Chateau d'Orleans............	1 00	2 00	Haut Sauterne, Souvenier	1 00	2 00
Hedgeside Cabernet..........	50	1 00	Chateau Yquem, Souvenier ...	1 25	2 50
" Sauterne............	50	1 00	Table D'Hote, Souvenier	75	1 25
Schramsberger Riesling.......	50	1 00	Margaux, Souvenier	1 00	2 00
Inglenook Burgundy..........	50	1 00	Medoc, Souvenier	1 00	2 00
" Riesling............	50	1 00	Naglee Brandy................		4 00
" Sauturne...........	50	1 00	Sunny Slope Port..........	75	1 50
Everett Ranch Zinfandel......	30	50	Palace Hotel Port.............	50	1 00
" Carrignan	35	60	Palace Hotel Sherry..........	50	1 00
Las Palmas Claret............	40	75			

Champagnes.

	Pts.	Qts.		Pts.	Qts.
Perrier Jouet, Special........	2 50	4 50	G. H. Mumm & Co., Extra Dry....	2 50	4 50
" Brut..............	2 50	4 50	Pommery & Greno Sec.........	2 50	4 50
Moet & Chandon, White Seal..	2 50	4 50	Veuve Clicquot, Dry.........	2 50	4 50
Moet & Chandon, Brut Imperial.	2 50	5 00	L. Roederer, Carte Blanche ...	2 50	4 50
Dry Monopole, Heidsieck & Co...	2 50	4 50	L. Roederer, Grand Vin Sec...	2 50	4 50
Jules Mumm & Co., Grand Sec..	2 50	4 50	L. Roederer, Brut............	2 50	4 50
Geo. Goulet, Extra Dry......	2 50	4 50	Ruinart Vin Brut, 1884.......	2 50	4 50
Gold Lack, Deutz & Gelderman..	2 50	4 50	Delbec & Co., Extra Dry......	2 50	4 50
Royal Berton Sec.............	2 50	4 50			

Clarets.

	Pts.	Qts.		Pts.	Qts.
St. Julien....................	0 50	1 00	Pontet Canet A. De Luze & Fils....		2 50
St. Julien, Barton & Guestier..	75	1 00	Pontet Canet 1874 Cuvillier & Frère	75	3 50
Chateau Leoville, A. De Luze &			Pauillac, 1881, Cuvillier & Frère..		1 50
Fils.......................	1 25	2 50	Chat. Beycheville, 1874 "	1 25	2 50
Chateau Leoville 1874 A De Luze & Fils		3 00	Chat. Larose, 1870. "	1 50	3 00
Chateau Giscours 1874 " "		4 00	Ducru Beau., 1881, Bar. & Guestier	1 25	2 50
Chateau Haut Brion 1874 " "		4 00	Chat. Laugoa, 1874, "	1 50	3 00
Chat. Paveil Marg., A. De Luze & Fils		3 00	Chat. Lafite, 1874 A De Luze & Fils		4 00
Chat. Paveil Marg. 1874 "		4 00	Chat. Le Terte...............		1 50
....			Chat.Latour1870, Barton & Guestier	2 00	4 00

Hungarian Wines.

Chateau Palugyay, red		2 00	Chateau Palugyay, white......		2 00

Italian Wines.

Chianti, Giorgio Gigliolt......		1 50	Barolo, Fratelli Cora.........		2 00

Sauternes.

Barsac Sauterne, 1878, Bar & Guestier	1 00	2 00	Château d' Yquem, Lur–Saluces	2 00	4 00
Haut Sauterne, A. De Luze & Fils.	1 25	2 50	Sauterne, Cuvillier & Frère ...		2 00
Graves, Nartigue & Bigourdan......		1 50	Chateau La Tour Blanche, C & F.		4 00

Burgundies.

Chablis, white, Cuvillier & Frere	1 50	3 00	Clos de Vougeot..............	2 00	4 00
			Chambertin..................	1 50	3 00

Hocks.

Königin Victoria Berg G. M. Pabstmann		4 00	Hochheimer, G. M. Pabstmann		2 00
Schloss Johanisberger, G. M. Pabstmann		3 50	Steinwein in Boxbeutel G. M. Pabstmann		3 00
Steinberger Cabinet, G. M. Pabstmann..		3 50	Liebfraumilch...............		2 00
Niersteiner..................		2 00	Deidesheimer................		2 00

Sparkling Hocks.

Moselle, Henkell & Co........	1 75	3 50	Johannisberger, Henkell & Co..	2 00	4 00

Sherries.

Montibello...................	1 00	2 00	No. 1 Extra, Private Stock....	1 25	2 50
Amontillado.................	1 75	3 00	Isabella.....................	2 00	4 00

Madeira.

No. 1 Extra—Private Stock	2 00	4 00	London Dock, Old Private Stock.	1 25	2 50
			Sanderman Port..............	1 75	3 00

Port.

Liqueurs, Etc.

Anisette, Marie, Brizard & Roger ..		3 00	Getreide Kümmel..............	2 00
Absinthe, Superieure		3 00	Creme de Menthe.............	3 00
Chartreuse, Green or Yellow		5 00	Maraschino..................	2 50
Kirschwasser..................		2 50	Benedictine..................	5 00
BRANDIES			**WHISKIES**	
Fine Champagne Brandy Reserve 1870,			Hermitage 1882..............	2 50
Cuvillier & Frère		5 00	Old Bourbon.................	2 00
Grande Fine Champagne Brandy,			Old Private Stock Bourbon....	2 50
1860, Cuvillier & Frère		6 00	Old Rye, Private Stock	2 00
Jas. Hennessy & Co., Cognac...		5 00	Royal Oak Rye, 1881.........	2 50
La Grande Marque 1872		4 00	Scotch, Vice-Regal Blend.....	2 50
Old Private Stock		5 00	Irish, Old, Fine.............	2 50

Malt Liquors, Etc.

Pabst Blue Ribbon Beer.......	0 30	0 60	Belfast Ginger Ale...........	35
Lager Beer all brands........	25	50	Merits Sparkling Cider.......	50	75
English Ale all brands	40	75	Apollinaris Water...........	25	50
" Porter "	40	75	Carlsbad....................		75
Atchison Scotch Ale..........	40	75	Mineral Waters all brands ...	25	50
S. F. Ale...................	30	60	Schwechat Beer, A. Dreher, Vienna		75
" Porter............	30	60			

CORKAGE, PER BOTTLE (CHAMPAGNE), $1 00
CORKAGE, PER BOTTLE (STILL WINES), 50c

RIDING IN SAFETY
CAFÉ ROYAL, LONDON

A dinner was given at the Café Royal in October 1895 by Mr John Kemp Starley to celebrate the tenth anniversary of the Rover bicycle. The first Rover cycle was introduced in 1884; this was a tricycle, which had to be propelled by hand and foot. Then in 1885 John Starley invented the safety bicycle, an invention which revolutionized the bicycle world.

At the time, the most common type of bicycle was the penny farthing, with an enormous front wheel and tiny back wheel, which was not a very stable machine. John Starley's invention had wheels almost the same size and rear-wheel drive with a chain, and was much more stable and comfortable. The days of the penny farthings were numbered, and by the end of the 1890s bicycles built according to the Rover's principles were the norm. The new bicycle was a big success. In 1908 the bicycles won every race in the Olympic games. John Starley died in 1901, but the company went on to develop a Rover motorcycle, the first machine having a 2.5hp engine manufactured by another company. This led Rover into the car manufacturing business in 1904.

The menu includes many rich dishes, including the heavily garnished consommé Sarah Bernhardt, named after the famous actress, turbot in sauce, and puff-pastry cases filled with a mixture of foie gras, tongue, truffles and mushrooms in a Madeira sauce. Smelts are tiny delicate white fish.

Menu for the dinner given at the Café Royal in October 1895 by Mr John Kemp Starley to celebrate the tenth anniversary of the Rover bicycle.

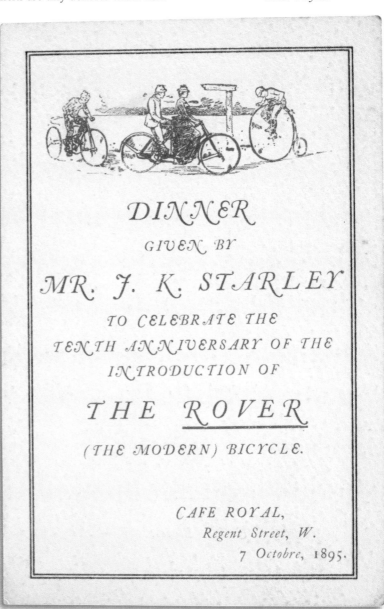

Above: The Rover safety bicycle, invented by John Starley in 1885.

VINS.

Sherry.

———

Wackenheim.

———

A. Bonvalot.

———

Dagonet Brut, 1884.

———

Palus de Cantenac, 1881.

———

Café et Liqueurs.

MENU.

Hors d'Œuvre variés.

Consommé Sarah Bernhardt.   Crême Dubarry.

Filets de Turbotin Mornay.
Pommes Nature.
Eperlans Colbert.

Bouchées Montglas.

Aloyau de Bœuf Jardinière.
Pommes Rissolées.   Haricots Verts.

Poularde à l'Ivoire.

Punch Nicols.

Perdreau rôti.
Salade.

Bombe Napolitaine.   Génoise Historiée.

Fromage.   Dessert.

MENU

Hors d'Oeuvres	Sauté Potatoes
Clear Soup Garnished	Green Beans
with Chicken Quenelles,	
Crayfish Tails, Tapioca and	Poached Chicken
Beef Marrow	Garnished with
Cream of Cauliflower	Mushrooms
Soup	and Chicken Dumplings,
	in a Cream Sauce
Fillet of Turbot in Cheese	
Sauce	Punch
Boiled Potatoes	
Smelts Fried in Egg and	Roast Partridge
Breadcrumbs	Salad
Puff Pastry Cases Filled	Neapolitan Ice Cream
with Foie Gras, Pickled	Mould
Tongue, Truffles and	Genoa Cake Decorated
Mushrooms in a Madeira-	with Flowers
Flavoured Sauce	Cheese
	Dessert
Sirloin of Beef with Fresh	
Vegetables	

Three Victorian bicycle riders in 1897.

ANNIVERSARY OF THE DUNLOP TYRE

Hotel Cecil, London

A celebration dinner was given at the Hotel Cecil on 19 November 1909 by the Pneumatic Tyre Industry. The celebration was for the 21st anniversary of the pneumatic tyre, patented by John Boyd Dunlop in 1888.

Dunlop was recognized as the inventor of the first practical pneumatic tyre (a tyre made of reinforced rubber and filled with compressed air). His patent for a bicycle tyre was granted in 1888. However, Robert William Thomson invented the actual first vulcanized rubber pneumatic tyre. Thomson patented his pneumatic tyre in 1845. His invention worked well but was costly and did not catch on. Dunlop's tyre did, and so he received the most recognition.

The first motor vehicle specifically designed for the pneumatic tyre took part in the Paris to Bordeaux race in 1895. After the round trip of 720 miles (1,159km) the Daimler finished ninth in a field of 42. From that event the simple tyre has developed in many directions, from bicycles to tractors and cars and even Formula 1 racing cars.

The Hotel Cecil, which was opened in 1896, was the largest in Europe and had 1,029 bedrooms, with two basement floors covering the complete area of the hotel.

TOASTS

"THE KING"

Proposed by - - - - The Chairman

* * *

"THE QUEEN, THE PRINCE & PRINCESS OF WALES,
and other members of the Royal Family"

Proposed by - - - - The Chairman

* * *

"THE PNEUMATIC TYRE INDUSTRY"

Proposed by - Arthur J. Walter, Esq., K.C.
Reply by - - - Harvey Du Cros, Esq., J.P.

* * *

"OUR INTERNATIONAL GUESTS"

Proposed by - - - - Julian Orde, Esq.
Reply by - - - Chevalier René de Knyff

* * *

"THE CHAIRMAN"

Proposed by - - C. Vernon Pugh, Esq., J.P.

MENU

WINES

Pale Sherry

Hockheimer

Château Mouton
Rothschild, 1896

Champagnes:
Bollinger & Co., 1904
George Goulet, 1900

Cockburn's
Old Tawny

Liqueurs and
Minerales

Huîtres Natives
Saumon Fumé

Tortue Claire

Suprême de Sole Polignac

Ris de Veau Royal

Carré d'Agneau à la Broche
Champignons   Haricot Verts
Pommes au Beurre

Sorbet au Grand Marnier

Faisan Flanqué de Mauviettes
Salade Capucin

Jambon d'York au Madère

Mandarines de Nice Glacée

Petits Fours

Dessert

Café Noir

One floor housed a grill room and dining room, smoking room and American bar, barber's saloon and telegraph room. The other floor housed the magnificent ballroom. The hotel finally closed its doors in 1930.

This is a long menu with many rich dishes, relieved halfway through with a liqueur sorbet to refresh the palate.

The pheasant dish must have been spectacular, the pheasants surrounded by larks (*mauviettes* is the French name for plump larks). The lark is said to have very delicate flesh, and in France lark pâté was greatly esteemed. Very few diners would dream of eating songbirds now, but they were less ecologically aware in those days.

THE
PNEUMATIC·TYRE
MAJORITY
CELEBRATION
19ᵀᴴ NOVEMBER
1909.

MENU

Oysters
Smoked Salmon

Clear Turtle Soup

Fillet of Sole in a Cream Sauce
with Mushrooms

Veal Sweetbreads in a Cream Sauce

Spit-Roasted Loin of Lamb
Mushrooms, Green Beans
Potatoes in Butter

Sorbet Grand Marnier

Pheasant Accompanied by Larks
Hare Salad

York Ham in Madeira Sauce

Iced Mandarin Oranges
Pastries
Dessert
Black Coffee

Charles Duryea was one of the pioneers of early automobiles and first built a car in 1893. He is seen here c1900 in one of the first cars ever to be equipped with pneumatic tyres.

149

CLARIDGE'S
HOTEL

HORSE OF THE YEAR SHOW

CLARIDGE'S, LONDON

A superb Pre-Raphaelite design adorns this Claridge's menu of 1912. The occasion was the Horse of the Year Show at Olympia, which ran from 17–29 June. This menu comes from the week before, when London would be filling up with judges and competitors.

Claridge's in Mayfair, London, is one of England's great institutions, an old-established hotel in the grand style. It is famous for its Art Deco style and its Victorian guest rooms, all recently restored.

It was established in 1812 when James Minart first opened a hotel in Brook Street. By 1838 he owned a row of five houses, knocked through to make a big hotel. The Great Exhibition of 1851 brought an influx of important visitors, including the Grand Duke Alexander of Russia, who stayed at the hotel.

Next door was another hotel run by William and Marianne Claridge. In 1854 they bought Minart's hotel, so that Claridge now owned a whole row of houses to the corner of the block. The seal of approval came when Queen Victoria came to visit the Empress Eugénie of France, who made Claridge's her winter quarters in 1860.

Another change in its fortunes came in 1894 when the hotel was bought by Richard d'Oyly Carte. He demolished the existing hotel and rebuilt the present building, reopening in 1898. The new hotel became a favourite society venue and was very popular with visiting royalty. It really came into its own after World War I, when many aristocrats sold their London homes as it was too expensive to keep up a house that was only used once a year, to entertain during the London Season. They discovered that it was much cheaper, and just as socially acceptable, to rent a suite at Claridge's.

In modern times Claridge's continued to be fashionable with the rich and famous, particularly exiled royalty, who often took up permanent residence. In 1941 the exiled King Peter of Yugoslavia came to stay permanently at Claridge's, and his son Crown Prince Alexander was born in Suite 212 in 1945. It has also become traditional for visiting statesmen to return British hospitality by hosting a banquet for the Queen at Claridge's.

Today Claridge's is a five-star de luxe hotel, well-placed for the expensive shops of Bond Street and Knightsbridge. It is attracting a new clientele of the trendy young as well as elder statesmen, business tycoons and royalty.

The 1912 menu is lavish by modern standards and includes the best of everything. We don't know what sole *à la Turque* is, but it may be sole served with rice pilaf or a spiced sauce. French salt meadow lamb is renowned for its flavour, and ducks from Nantes were also held in high esteem. The dessert is some kind of apple dish, but we have no idea what it was – some special creation of the chef, no doubt.

A superb Pre-Raphaelite design adorns the cover of this Claridge's menu from 1912.

MENU

Hors-d'Oeuvres
Clear Soup Garnished with Tapioca,
Moulded Custard Shapes and Chervil Cream Soup

Fillet of Sole

Saddle of Salt Meadow Lamb with Vegetables
Creamed Potatoes

Chicken Breast

Braised Duck with Cherries
Salad

Artichoke with Cream Sauce

Apples

Sweetmeats

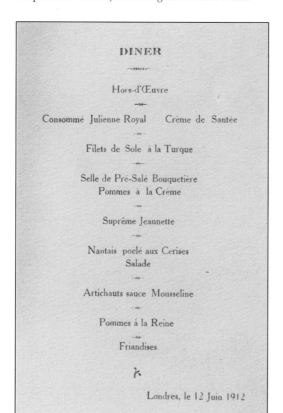

DINER

Hors-d'Œuvre

Consommé Julienne Royal   Crème de Santée

Filets de Sole à la Turque

Selle de Pré-Salé Bouquetière
Pommes à la Crème

Suprême Jeannette

Nantais poelé aux Cerises
Salade

Artichauts sauce Mousseline

Pommes à la Reine

Friandises

ᚸ

Londres, le 12 Juin 1912

DINING IN PARADISE
ROYAL HAWAIIAN HOTEL, HONOLULU

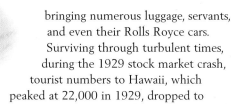

This menu is from the Royal Hawaiian Hotel, Honolulu, in 1929, at the height of its popularity. The elegant dining room is shown on the cover of the menu. Events of the day included coconut tree climbing by Hawaiian boys and activities included surfing, deep-sea fishing, hiking, riding, polo and tennis.

The hotel opened on 1 February 1927 with a gala celebration for over 1,000 guests, costing $10 per person, and Princess Kawananakoa was the first registered guest. The owners built it as a luxury hotel for Matson Line ocean liner passengers, and it initiated a new era in luxurious resorts in Hawaii for the growing number of wealthy tourists. Queen Ka'ahumanu had her summer palace in the coconut grove where the 'Pink Palace', as it was known, was built.

The hotel cost four million dollars and took one and a half years to build. It was built in Spanish-Moorish style, with cupolas that resembled bell towers. This style was popular in the period, influenced by screen star Rudolph Valentino, who starred in films such as the *Four Horsemen of the Apocalypse* and *Blood and Sand*. The architects were Warren and Wetmore of New York, who were well known in hotel design.

In those early days, guests would come for a long stay

bringing numerous luggage, servants, and even their Rolls Royce cars. Surviving through turbulent times, during the 1929 stock market crash, tourist numbers to Hawaii, which peaked at 22,000 in 1929, dropped to 10,000 by 1932 and did not reach 22,000 again until 1936.

Then came World War II with barbed wire installed along Waikiki Beach. In January 1942, the hotel was leased to the Navy as a rest and recreation centre for those serving in the Pacific Fleet, and at the end of the war in October 1945 the hotel was given back to Matson Line, which re-opened it to the public in February 1947 after spending nearly two million dollars on its refurbishment.

In 1929 they offered an extensive menu for lunch, from broiled ulua (a large tasty reef fish) to pressed calf head with sauce *gribiche*, a vinaigrette sauce with chopped hard-boiled egg, capers, gherkins and herbs. There was a choice of 12 desserts and 14 different cheeses. The tongue is described as '*écarlate*', which just means scarlet. *Blanquette* of veal is a veal stew, the sauce thickened with eggs and cream. The desserts include two French dishes – a chestnut ice cream and a cherry-flavoured ice cream.

ARRANGEMENTS CAN BE MADE AT THE FRONT OFFICE FOR HAWAIIAN SURFING, DEEP SEA FISHING, HIKING, RIDING POLO AND TENNIS, OR ANY OTHER SPORTS WHICH YOU MAY ENJOY.

THE WAIALAE GOLF COURSE AT WAIALAE BEACH OFFERS YOU THE FINEST 18 HOLE GOLF LINKS IN THE ISLAND. GREEN FEE $2.00 ON WEEK DAYS, $2.50 ON SATURDAYS, SUNDAYS & HOLIDAYS A COMPLETELY EQUIPPED CLUBHOUSE. WEEKLY DINNER-DANCE EVERY FRIDAY SPECIAL PARTIES ARRANGED.

A VISIT TO THE HAWAIIAN PINEAPPLE COMPANY'S CANNERY CAN BE ARRANGED PLEASE SEE THE CLERK, AT THE FRONT OFFICE.

THERE ARE A NUMBER OF BEAUTIFUL AND INTERESTING AUTOMOBILE TRIPS INCLUDING A TRIP AROUND THE ISLAND OF OAHU WHICH MAY BE ARRANGED FOR BY APPLYING TO THE TAXI AGENT IN THE LOBBY.

EVENTS OF THE DAY

Coconut Tree Climbing by Hawaiian Boys - 2:30 p. m.
Afternoon Tea will be served at 4 on the Coconut Grove Lanai.

SUNSET SERENADE;
Joe Kamakau's Hawaiians and Royal Hawaiian Girls Glee Club 6:30 p. m.

ROYAL HAWAIIAN BAND CONCERT - - 7:30 p. m.

Royal Hawaiian Glee Club with Hula and Songs by Mary Kackanson's Tiny Hawaiians, Princess Kinini and Ululani Robinson - - 9:00 p. m.

TEMPERATURES TODAY AIR 78 WATER 79

Menu
LUNCHEON
THURSDAY, AUGUST 8, 1929

Green Onions   Pickled Lamb Tongue   Sweet Gherkins
Salad Charcutiere   Herring Delicatesse

SOUP
Consomme Nature   Chicken Mulligatawny
Chicken Broth in Cup, Hot or Cold

FISH
Broiled Ulua, Paprika Butter, Chip Potatoes

ENTREES
Shirred Egg Cluny
Calf Liver Saute, Smothered Onions
Blanquette of Veal with Mushrooms a l'Ancienne
Vegetable Plate with Shrimps Creole
Spaghetti Napolitaine

SALAD SUGGESTION - DALILA

FROM THE GRILL
Broiled English Mutton Chop,
Chip Potatoes

FRESH VEGETABLES
Garden Spinach au Jus   Poi   Hubbard Squash au Gratin
Fried Zucchini   Carrots in Cream   Boiled Rice
Potatoes—Baked, Boiled, Mashed or Hashed Brown

COLD BUFFET
Consomme in Jelly   Sliced Chicken   Chicken Salad   York Ham in Jelly
Essence of Tomato   Chicken Loaf   Beef Tongue Ecarlate
Pressed Calf Head Sauce Gribiche   Veal Loaf, Potato Salad
Pressed Chicken and Virginia Ham in Jelly
Home Made Head Cheese, Pickled Beets
Spiced Loin of Pork, Cabbage Slaw
Prime Ribs of Island Beef

SALAD
Tropical   Chicory, French Dressing   Potato
"A bit of sweet makes the meal complete"
DESSERTS & ICE CREAM
Patisserie Francaise   Fresh Apple Pie   Cocoanut Custard Pie
Blackberry Meringue Pie   Deep Dish Cabinet Pudding
Chocolate, Vanilla & Coffee Cup Custard
French Vanilla   Coffee   Peach   Chocolate
Coupe aux Marrons   Parfait Maraschino

FRESH FRUIT
Pineapple   Banana   Oranges   Cherries   Cantaloupe   Plums
Water-melon   Peaches   Grapes   Casaba-melon   Solo Papaia
Persian-melon   Honeydew-melon   Pears

CHEESE
New American   Double Cream   Camembert   Swiss   Swiss Gruyere
Roquefort   Neufchatel   Pimento   Schabzieger   Cottage
Gorgonzola   Pineapple   Cheddar   Trappiste
AFRICAN DATES   NUTS & RAISINS
COFFEE   TEA   MILK
Any dishes ordered that are not on the Menu will be charged extra.
Room Service 25c extra each person.

The menu cover for the Royal Hawaiian Hotel shows a vignette of the elegant dining room, while inside it lists sports, pastimes and events of the day, including coconut tree climbing, a glee club serenade and an evening concert.

DINING AT THE HEART OF THE BIG APPLE

THE EMPIRE STATE BUILDING, NEW YORK

GENUINE STEEL GRAVURE

EMPIRE STATE BUILDING
NEW YORK

TALLEST STRUCTURE IN THE WORLD
1248 FEET HIGH   102 STORIES

Soups and Appetizers

Fruit Cup	20c	Fresh Fruit	35c
Beef or Chicken Bouillon			15c
Special Soup			20c
Pineapple Juice			20c
Tomato Juice Cocktail			20c

Salads

Pineapple & Cream Cheese	50c	Potato & Sardine	65c
Hearts of Lettuce	50c	Crabflake Salad with Egg & Tomato & Russian Dressing	80c
Tuna Fish	70c	Potato, Tomato & Egg	80c
Salmon Salad	70c		
Potato Salad	50c	Chicken Salad	85c
Tomato Salad	60c	Asparagus & Egg	75c
Fruit Salad	70c	Sliced Ham & Potato Salad with Tomato	80c
Egg Salad	60c		
Shrimp Salad	60c	Tomato Stuffed with Chicken	90c
Harvard Salad	75c		
Egg Salad & Sliced Tomatoes	75c	Assorted Cold Cuts	80c
		With Chicken	95c
		Tomato with Shrimp	80c

Roll and Butter served with Salads.....5c

Sandwiches

Peanut Butter	30c	Chicken Salad	70c
American Cheese	40c	Ham & Tomato	60c
Swiss Cheese	40c		
Cream Cheese & Jelly	35c	Combination	65c
		Sliced Chicken	70c
Tuna Fish	50c		
Baked Ham	55c	Liverwurst	40c
Sliced Egg	40c	Smithfield-Ham & Chopped Egg	60c
Salmon	50c		
Shrimp Salad	50c	Sardine	50c
Tomato & Lettuce	40c		
Cream Cheese & Olive	35c	Cream Cheese on Date & Nut Bread	40c
Cream Cheese & Nut	40c	Chicken, Ham, & Tomato	90c

This priced menu from the Empire State Building in New York c1930 shows tuna fish salad at 70c, chicken salad at 85c, apple pie at 20c and a cup of coffee at 10c (how things have changed). It is not exactly *haute cuisine*, but the tourists were no doubt satisfied that it was good value for money. The building was officially opened on 1 May 1931 by President Herbert Hoover, who pressed a button in Washington, DC to turn on the lights.

The building is 1,248 feet (380m) in height, with 102 stories, and the site covers about 2 acres. A number of films have been made there, notably *King Kong* in 1933. Robert Armstrong stars as the adventurer Carl Denham, who leads a trip to the strange island to photograph the monster. Along for the trip is Ann Darrow (Fay Wray). King Kong falls in love with Ann Darrow, but at the end of the film King Kong meets his death on top of the Empire State Building. The scene is one of the most memorable in movie history.

Special 25c
Cinnamon Toast
(on Whole Wheat Raisin Bread)
Tea - Coffee - Milk

Special 35c
Toasted English Muffin
Jam or Marmalade
Tea - Coffee - Milk

Special 70c
Any 35c or 45c Sandwich
Small Ice Cream
Tea - Coffee - Milk

Special 80c
Salmon or Tuna Fish
& Vegetable Salad
Special Cake or Ice Cream
Tea - Coffee - Milk

Special 80c
Waldorf Salad
Cinnamon Toast
Cup Cake
Tea - Coffee - Milk

Special 80c
Assorted Sandwiches
Ice Cream
Tea - Coffee - Milk

Special 80c
Stuffed Egg
Combination Salad
Mayonnaise Dressing
Roll and Butter
Ice Cream
Tea - Coffee - Milk

Special 85c
Fresh Fruit Salad
with Celery
Buttered Nut Bread
Tea - Coffee - Milk

Roll or Bread with Butter____5c

Special 95c
Fruit Salad and Assorted
Canapes
Ice Cream or Special Cake
Tea - Coffee - Milk

No Change or Substitutions on Specials
Iced Tea - Iced Coffee on 75c and 85c Specials Only
Iced Tea - Iced Coffee on all others - 5c extra
Only One Cup of Coffee per Customer

WINES AND LIQUORS
SEE WINE LIST

Desserts

Apple Pie	20c	Cheese & Crackers	25c
Special Layer Cake	15c	Date and Nut Bread with Butter	15c
Special Pie	20c	Saltines	10c
Pie a la' mode	30c	Social Tea	10c

Beverages

Coffee - Cup 10c   Iced - 20c   Per Pot____25c
Orange Pekoe Tea-Cup 10c   Iced-20c   Per Pot__25c
Hot Chocolate ____15c   Iced _____20c
Milk - (Bottle)_____10c
Coca Cola _____10c   Lemon and Lime sm. 10c
Large Coca Cola____15c   Lemon and Lime lg. 15c
Root Beer _____10c   Large Root Beer____15c

Fresh Fruit Drinks
(in Season)

Grape Fruit Juice	20c	Lemonade	25c
Grape Juice	20c	Limeade	25c
Lime Rickey	25c	Orangeade	25c
Grape Juice Lime-ade	25c	Grape Fruit Juice Limeade	25c
Orange Juice	25c		

Fountain Drinks

Milk Shake—Any Flavor _____20c
Ice Cream Sodas—Any Flavor_____20c
Sundaes _____25c
Large Plate Ice Cream 25c—Small_____15c
Malted Milk—All Flavors ____25c—With Egg____30c
Frosted Drinks—All Flavors ____25c—With Egg____30c
Milk Floats—All Flavors_____25c—With Egg____30c

AMERICAN
Culinary Festival

CELEBRATING AMERICAN CUISINE
THE CARLTON TOWER HOTEL, LONDON

This priced menu is from the Carlton Tower Hotel, London, for an American Culinary Festival in 1964. It features the proud chef with his array of fine foods, a motif which has adorned the menu cover of the world-renowned Oak Room of the New York Plaza for many years. The executive chef of the Oak Room, Mr André René, represented the US at the Hotel Olympia exhibition in London in January 1964.

The menu offers dishes from different regions such as New England, Middle Atlantic states, Pennsylvania Dutch, Creole country and the Far West. New England is known for its long winters. Early settlers needed warming, hardy food and developed recipes from the foods that were plentiful: corn, pumpkin and beans, roast turkey and oyster stew were typical fare. Middle Atlantic dishes can be traced to the early settlers in Virginia and the cosmopolitan travellers to New York. This region features marvellous chicken dishes, smoked and cured hams, crabs and oysters, hot breads and pecan desserts. Pennsylvania Dutch has authentic recipes with distinctive ingredients such as dried apples and schnitz apple butter, brown sugar and molasses, pickled cabbage, with plenty of spices and sweet and sour relishes. Creole country cookery was born in New Orleans, Louisiana, which was first ruled by the French and then the Spanish, and influenced by immigrants from the West Indies. These influences blend together to produce a unique cuisine with dishes such as oyster, shrimp and crab gumbo. The Far West has an abundance of quality beef cattle, ideal for steaks and ribs, while the fertile land of California produces marvellous fruits and vegetables, with fish from the rivers of the northwest and the Pacific Ocean.

A MENU OF
American Regional Cuisine

Suggestions for Cocktails

Jim Beam Manhattan 7/6	Old Fashioned 9/-	Martini 5/-	Whiskey Sour 6/6

Appetizers

NEW ENGLAND
New England Clam Chowder 5/-
Gloucester Codfish Balls 4/6

MIDDLE ATLANTIC STATES
Epicurean Oyster Cocktail 17/6
Snapper Soup 7/-

PENNSYLVANIA DUTCH
Flaish Un Kais (small, meat-filled pastry) .. 4/6
Philadelphia Pepper Pot Soup 5/-

CREOLE COUNTRY
Creole Crab Gumbo 6/-
Oysters à la Rockefeller 21/-

FAR WEST
Frosted California Fruit Cup 4/6
Iced Avocado Soup 5/-
Alaska King Crab Cocktail 10/-

For your Enjoyment

We are pleased to serve a selection of breads—Corn Scones, Pecan Rolls, Banana Bread and Sally Lunn Bread.

The Seven Sweet and Seven Sour Relishes of the Pennsylvania Dutch region are also being served during our Festival.

American Wines

CHAMPAGNE
Charles Fournier, New York, Gold Seal   1960   50/-

RED
Cabernet Sauvignon   1960   32/6
San Martin, Estate Bottled, Beaulieu
Vineyard, California

Pinot Noir   1960   27/6
Paul Masson,
Estate Bottled, California

WHITE
White Pinot   1960   32/6
Inglenook Vineyard, Estate Bottled,
California

Emerald Dry   1961   27/6
Riesling, Paul Masson,
Estate Bottled, California

Entrees

NEW ENGLAND
Whole Maine Lobster Boiled or Broiled with Steamed Clams, Drawn Butter and French Fried Potatoes (*Two Covers*) 45/-

New England Boiled Dinner Specially prepared Brisket of Beef, Cabbage, Potatoes, Carrots, Onions and Turnips 22/6

PENNSYLVANIA DUTCH
Schnitz Un Knepp Smoked Ham cooked with Dry Apples and Small Stuffed Dumplings 21/-

Hairnhutter Rinsflaish Mit Donkes Moravian Beef with Gravy, Pickled Red Cabbage and Dutch Beans 21/-

MIDDLE ATLANTIC STATES
Chesapeake Crab Imperial A Baked Casserole with Seasoning of Sherry and Paprika 17/6

Brunswick Stew Tender Chicken slowly simmered with Potatoes, String Beans, Okra, Corn Kernels and Tomatoes 19/6

Baked Sugar-Cured Ham Virginia style with Green Beans, Bacon, Candied Yams and Spiced Peaches 21/-

Fried Chicken Maryland with Cream Gravy, Corn Fritters and String Beans 19/6

Rock Cornish Game Hen, Bird of Paradise A Roasted Cornish Hen with Stuffing served on Half Pineapple with Wild Rice 30/-

CREOLE COUNTRY
Pompano En Papillotte Poached Fillets of Pompano with Shrimp Stuffing, wrapped in Parchment and Baked, served with Stuffed Eggplant 17/6

Shrimp Jambalaya A Medley of Shrimp, Oysters, Ham, Chicken and Rice, served with Candied Louisiana Yams 21/-

FAR WEST
Broiled Porterhouse Steak served with a Western Herb Sauce, Baked Potato, Green Peas and Mushrooms (*Two Covers*) 55/-

Roast Prime Ribs of Beef served with Baked Potato, Sour Cream and Buttered Asparagus 22/6

Desserts

NEW ENGLAND
Fluffy Pumpkin Pie 4/-
Deep Dish Blueberry Pie 5/6
Frozen Rum Pudding 4/6

PENNSYLVANIA DUTCH
Shoo-Fly Pie (molasses in seasoned crumb shell) 3/-

MIDDLE ATLANTIC STATES
Lady Baltimore Cake 3/-
Southern Pecan Pie 5/-

CREOLE COUNTRY
Ambrosia (sugared orange slices with shredded fresh cocoanut) 3/6
Apricot Rum Whip 3/6

FAR WEST
Ice Cream Sundae, Santa Barbara 4/6
Old Fashioned Strawberry Shortcake 10/6

BEVERAGES
Coffee 2/6   Tea 2/6   Café Brûlot 6/6

PICTURE ACKNOWLEDGMENTS

INTRODUCTION
pages 6–7 © Mary Evans Picture Library

ROYAL WEDDINGS
page 8 © Hulton-Deutsch Collection/Corbis
page 10 top l. top r. bot © Mary Evans Picture Library
page 12 © Mary Evans Picture Library
page 13 b. © Massimo Listri/Corbis
page 22 © Hulton-Deutsch Collection/Corbis
page 24 © Bettmann/Corbis
page 26 © Brendan Beirne/Sygma/Corbis
page 29 © Bettmann/Corbis
page 31 © Graham Tim/Corbis Sygma

ROYAL BANQUETS
page 34 © Hulton-Deutsch Collection/Corbis
page 37 © Hulton-Deutsch Collection/Corbis
page 38 © Bettmann/Corbis
page 41 © Hulton-Deutsch Collection/Corbis

page 44 © Tim Graham/Corbis
page 45 t. © Hulton-Deutsch Collection/Corbis; b. © Hulton-Deutsch Collection/Corbis
page 47 t. © Eric and David Hosking/Corbis; b. © Hulton-Deutsch Collection/Corbis;
page 48 © Tim Graham/Corbis
page 49 © Mary Evans Picture Library
page 52 © Hulton-Deutsch Collection/Corbis

STATE BANQUETS
page 57 © Hulton-Deutsch Collection/Corbis
page 58 © Historical Picture Archive/Corbis
page 61 © Bettmann/Corbis
page 64 t. © Bettmann/Corbis; b. © Bettmann/Corbis
page 66 l. © Bettmann/Corbis; r. © Lester Lefkowitz/Corbis
page 69 t. © Bettmann/Corbis
page 70 © Tim Graham/Corbis
page 72 © Miroslaw Kaldunski

DINING AT SEA
page 77 © Bettmann/Corbis
page 79 t. © Underwood & Underwood/Corbis; b. and background © Bettmann/Corbis
page 81 © Hulton-Deutsch Collection/Corbis

BIRTHDAYS AND CELEBRATIONS
page 103 © Corbis
page 107 © Corbis
page 110 © Corbis
page 111 © Alain Noques/Sygma/Corbis

SPORTING EVENTS
page 115 © Peter Aprahamian/Corbis
page 120 © Hulton-Deutsch Collection/Corbis
page 123 © Bettmann/Corbis
page 127 © JP Laffont/Sygma/Corbis

DINING IN STYLE
page 146 © Mary Evans Picture Library
page 147 © Bettmann/Corbis
page 149 © Bettmann/Corbis